HANDS-ON
ROCKY MOUNTAINS

ART ACTIVITIES ABOUT ANASAZI, AMERICAN INDIANS, SETTLERS, TRAPPERS, AND COWBOYS

This book is dedicated to my brother, William (Bill) Rigby Young, Jr.
Though he missed his true century of exploring the West,
his adventure-seeking spirit prevailed in his shortened but legendary life.

Book design by Kinde Nebeker Design
Jim Tilly and Joni Sweetman - Art & International Productions
Edited by Victoria Hindley
Photographs by Laurel Casjens

Illustrated by Mary Simpson,
who also assisted with craft research, design,
production, and the testing of prototypes.

Other books by the author:

Published by Kits Publishing
Hands-on Celebrations **Hands-on Alaska**
(ISBN 0-9643177-4-5) (ISBN 0-9643177-3-7)

Published by Deseret Book
Hands-on Pioneers
(ISBN 1-57345-085-5)

KITS PUBLISHING
2359 East Bryan Ave.
Salt Lake City, Utah 84108
fax: 801-582-2540

© 1996 Yvonne Young Merrill

First Printing July 1996
Printed in Hong Kong

Library of Congress Catalog Card Number 96-94674

ISBN 0-9643177-2-9

HANDS-ON ROCKY MOUNTAINS

ART ACTIVITIES ABOUT ANASAZI, AMERICAN INDIANS, SETTLERS, TRAPPERS, AND COWBOYS

YVONNE Y. MERRILL

KITS PUBLISHING

THE TIME LINE

10,000 B.C. to 6500 B.C.
Paleoindian stone projectile tips are used to hunt mammoth and great bison. Gatherers appear in the Four Corners region.

6500 B.C. to 1500 B.C.
Archaic hunter-gatherers appear. The atlatl, a throwing board for spears, is introduced.

1500 B.C. to 500 A.D.
Anasazi Basketmakers I & II appear along with rock art, coiled and twined basketry, and agricultural products such as corn and squash.

500 A.D. to 750 A.D.
The era of the Anasazi Basketmaker III. Agriculture expands to include beans. The bow and arrow, plain gray pottery and kivas are introduced.

INTRODUCTION

The remarkable Rocky Mountain range extends north into Canada and south to the desert of the Southwest. The peaks divide the continent. The Continental Divide is the point where waters flow west to the Pacific Ocean or to eastern waterways. This challenging mountain spine impacted the frontier story we tell in this book.

The history of the Rocky Mountain West tells a rich story of survival and determination in beautiful, rugged country. Many groups have inhabited the area, some with the goal to simply survive from one season to the next, others with the dream of prosperity, and some individuals were drawn to the West by the hint of adventure. Pioneers, workers, and explorers traveled by horseback from Eastern cities. Others, who were fleeing from persecution, came in covered wagons, and still others trekked on foot, moving from one hunting ground to the next. Regardless of their origin and the motivation that drove them to the magnificent West, several common themes unite the fascinating people who headed west and thrived.

Each group, throughout many eras, found inspiration in the natural splendor of the mountain West. The five groups discussed in this book shared a sense of adventure, an inventive resourcefulness, and a commitment to skilled workmanship that showed in the beauty of common objects. Whether the season was hot and dry or snowy and cold, whether the land was characterized by sandy red rock or lush pine forest, the western people adapted. The groups that settled and thrived in the West were ordinary people doing extraordinary things.

You are invited to explore the world of the first Archaic peoples, their American Indian descendants, and groups of cowboys, settlers, and trappers. See how they used their imagination and abundant skills to tame the land and thrive from its bounty.

1400 A.D.
There are an estimated 5 to 25 million American Indians thriving on the continent.

1521 A.D. to 1776 A.D.
Cortés brings horses to the region. California is settled by the Spanish. Escalante explores the Southwest seeking a route to California and discovers the Grand Canyon.

1803 A.D. to 1805 A.D.
The Lewis and Clark expedition ends in the Pacific Northwest.

1825 A.D.
The first fur rendezvous takes place.

50 A.D. to 1300 A.D.
The Fremont people live in Utah.
The bow and arrow is used. Pottery and
agriculture are important features of daily
life. Villages are unoccupied by 1300 A.D.

750 A.D. to 1100 A.D.
The Pueblo Period of the Anasazi.
Pueblo Bonito is built in Chaco
Canyon. Cliff dwellings and stone
structures are constructed. Fine
black and white pottery is made.

1100 A.D. to 1300 A.D.
Impressive cliff dwellings and
great kivas are built.
Irrigation and surface flooding
are introduced. Villages are
unoccupied by 1300.

1300 A.D. to 1500 A.D.
Numic-speaking descendents
of the Shoshoni appear in the
region. The Navajo tribe appears
in the Four Corners area.

CONTENTS

1836 A.D. to 1847 A.D.
The last fur rendezvous takes place.
The Oregon trail is established. The
Mormons arrive in Utah.

1865 A.D.
The American Civil War
begins in 1861. The first cattle
drive to northern country
takes place.

1869 A.D.
The East-West railroad
is joined at Promontory Point,
Ogden, Utah.

1885
The last cattle drive to "feed lots"
takes place. The first American
Indians are placed on reservations.

3

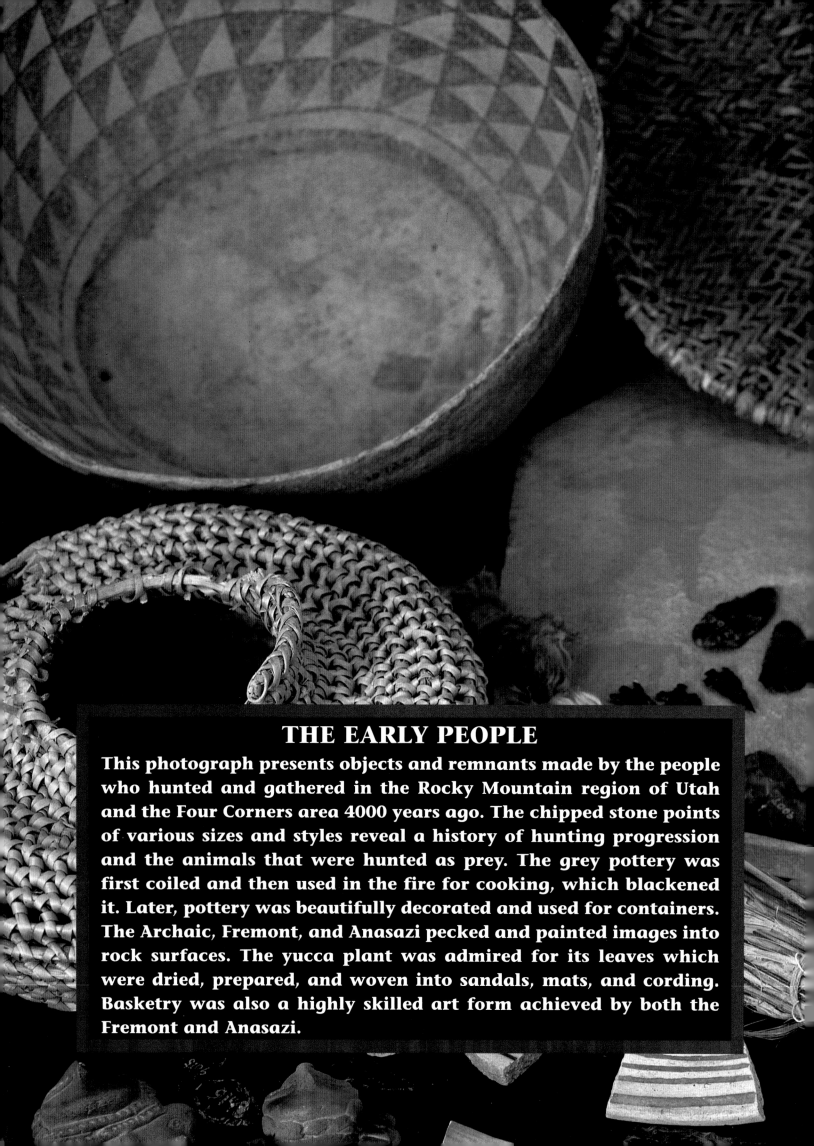

THE EARLY PEOPLE

This photograph presents objects and remnants made by the people who hunted and gathered in the Rocky Mountain region of Utah and the Four Corners area 4000 years ago. The chipped stone points of various sizes and styles reveal a history of hunting progression and the animals that were hunted as prey. The grey pottery was first coiled and then used in the fire for cooking, which blackened it. Later, pottery was beautifully decorated and used for containers. The Archaic, Fremont, and Anasazi pecked and painted images into rock surfaces. The yucca plant was admired for its leaves which were dried, prepared, and woven into sandals, mats, and cording. Basketry was also a highly skilled art form achieved by both the Fremont and Anasazi.

UTAH

Great Salt Lake

COLORADO

NEW MEXICO

ARIZONA

As early as 10,000 to 6500 B.C. the Paleoindian People in the southwestern region of the Rocky Mountains hunted the Bison antiquus and the mammoth. Their stone tools are almost the only evidence of their existence. Spear points chipped from stones are found throughout the area. Perhaps these sharp, wedge-shaped tips were made to fit the end of a "spear" and were changed depending on the animal being hunted.

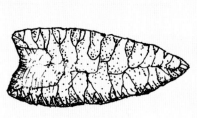

CLOVIS TIPS   FOLSOM TIPS   MAMMOTH   BISON ANTIQUUS

THE ARCHAIC PEOPLE

After the Ice Age, from 6500 to 1500 B.C. large animals disappeared and early people, thought of as hunter-gatherers, hunted antelope, deer, elk, and rabbits. They also ate berries, nuts, and roots. The invention and skilled use of the "throwing stick" called the *atlatl* had its first appearance with the Archaic hunters. The atlatl holds a spear and gives the weapon greater force and distance. Experts have also found evidence of crushed seeds, apparently used to make flour.

THE FREMONT PEOPLE

The Fremont people lived in the southwestern area of the Rocky Mountains in what is now Utah in approximately 700 A.D. (the same era as the Anasazi). Their living patterns were a combination of settled and nomadic. When settled, they lived in pit houses and maintained agriculture. Villages were either large or made of just a few dwellings. The Fremont dwellings were characterized by adobe mortar and shaped stone granaries. They grew gardens, made simple gray pottery or gray pots which have been blackened, and made leather moccasins. They also made small clay figures decorated with

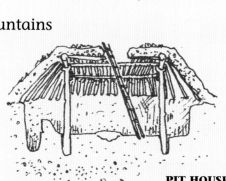

PIT HOUSE

necklaces and hair bobs. We aren't sure of their purpose, but the figurines might have been toys, objects of worship or ornamental objects. The Fremont culture peaked in the year 1300 and left evidence in northern Utah of several unoccupied agricultural sites. The fate of the Fremont people is a question archaeologists are still trying to solve. Were they forced out by newcomers? by drought? by disease?

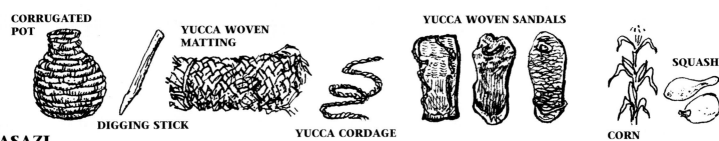

PEOPLE

CORRUGATED POT

DIGGING STICK

YUCCA WOVEN MATTING

YUCCA CORDAGE

YUCCA WOVEN SANDALS

CORN

SQUASH

ANASAZI

Anasazi is a Navajo word that means "ancient people that are not us." They are also referred to as "Ancestral Pueblo people" and "Hisatsenom" by the Hopi. They lived in the Four Corners region of Utah, Colorado, Arizona, and New Mexico. The earliest evidence of the Anasazi is dated 1500 B.C., what we refer to as the early Basketmaker people. Woven baskets, woven matting and cord, and digging sticks confirm that they were an agricultural people growing such items as corn and squash. They still used the atlatl for hunting. They also created pictographs and petroglyphs and by 500 A.D., the beginning of Basketmaker III era, they were making gray pottery and storing surplus food. Beans were grown, an important nutritional mainstay, beans improved health and increased life span. Kivas, or religious rooms, were made. An advance among this group, and the later Fremont people (750 A.D.), was the use of the bow and arrow which introduced the ability to hunt from a distance with accuracy and speed. Projectile points were now used as tips of arrows. The Fremont and the Anasazi people lived in pit houses during this time.

THE GREAT PUEBLO PERIOD

SHAPED STONE

The high point of the Anasazi culture, from 700 to 1300 A.D., is referred to as the Great Pueblo Period. There was much architectural innovation which culminated in the remarkable cliff dwellings of this period. For 1,000 years the Great Pueblo Anasazi inhabited the Rocky Mountain Southwest, developing irrigation and surface flooding in otherwise dry, rocky country. During this period we see the region's first shaped adobe stone buildings—circular rooms called kivas—built both above and below ground. Remains indicate these people painted their buildings yellow, black, and white. They gardened and cultivated fields; and they designed fine pottery in black and white. They also built what might have been sacred places. Some Great Pueblo sites are located in Hovenweep, Utah; Mesa Verde, Colorado; and Pueblo Bonito in Chaco Canyon, New Mexico.

By 1300 A.D. the Anasazi had left most of their homes. Perhaps deforestation caused a combination of erosion and vulnerability. It is speculated that raiding enemies, pests, and disease from poor sanitation contributed to the downfall. Trouble within the group may have caused civil war. By 1200 the Numic people make an appearance and by 1500 the Navajo appear. The Hopi, Zuni, and the 18 tribes of the Rio Grande Pueblos are most likely the living descendants of the Anasazi.

MESA VERDE

PUEBLO BONITO

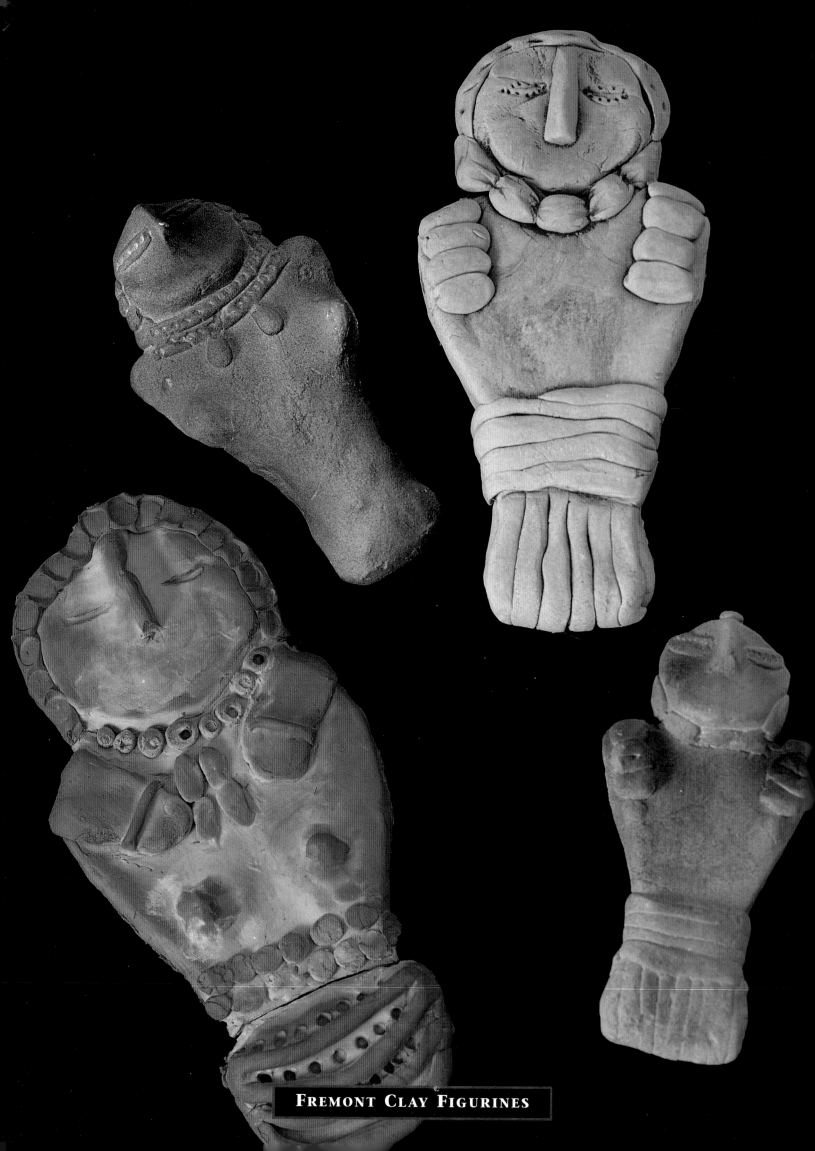

FREMONT CLAY FIGURINES

FREMONT CLAY FIGURINE

Materials: homemade baker's clay or commercial self-hardening clay; tools like wooden craft sticks; pencil points and water for easier molding of clay.

1. Separate a lump of clay about the size of a lemon. Flatten it into a rectangle that is 4 to 6 inches long. The bottom of the figure will be about one-third of entire length.

2. Form the following parts separately: a raised nose, thin eyes, and tiny balls and pendants for the necklace and clothing details. Attach with a dab of water.

3. Mold some figurines with stubby arms and bobs on the top and sides of the head for hair. Use clay coils to decorate the bottom of the figure.

4. Allow clay figurine to air dry on a rack for about 24 hours.

From 500 B.C. to 1300 A.D. the Anasazi people were living in the Four Corners region. The Fremont people lived north and west of the Colorado river in Utah from 700 to 1300 A.D. They hunted wild game and raised corn, beans, and squash.

They fashioned these small, intriguing figurines from the native gray clay. These may have been toys, ornaments or charms used to encourage good harvests.

CORRUGATED POTTERY

CORRUGATED POTTERY

Materials: baker's clay, Plasticine™, or commercial self-hardening clay.

1. Make pencil-sized coils by rolling clay.

2. Create a flat base with your coils, pinching the coils together as you build.

3. Add more coils to build up the sides of your corrugated pot until it is the height you want.

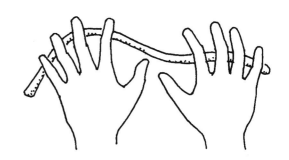

Anasazi people made pottery with similar techniques to those described here. One thousand years ago, they dug up gray clay, rolled it into pencil thin rolls and pinched the coils together to make pots. The inside was flattened using hands and tools. The outside was marked with wavy lines formed by the potter's fingers.

This kind of textured pottery is called corrugated pottery. Corrugated pottery was used for common needs such as carrying food and water and cooking. It was seldom decorated and turned a deep black when used in the cooking fire.

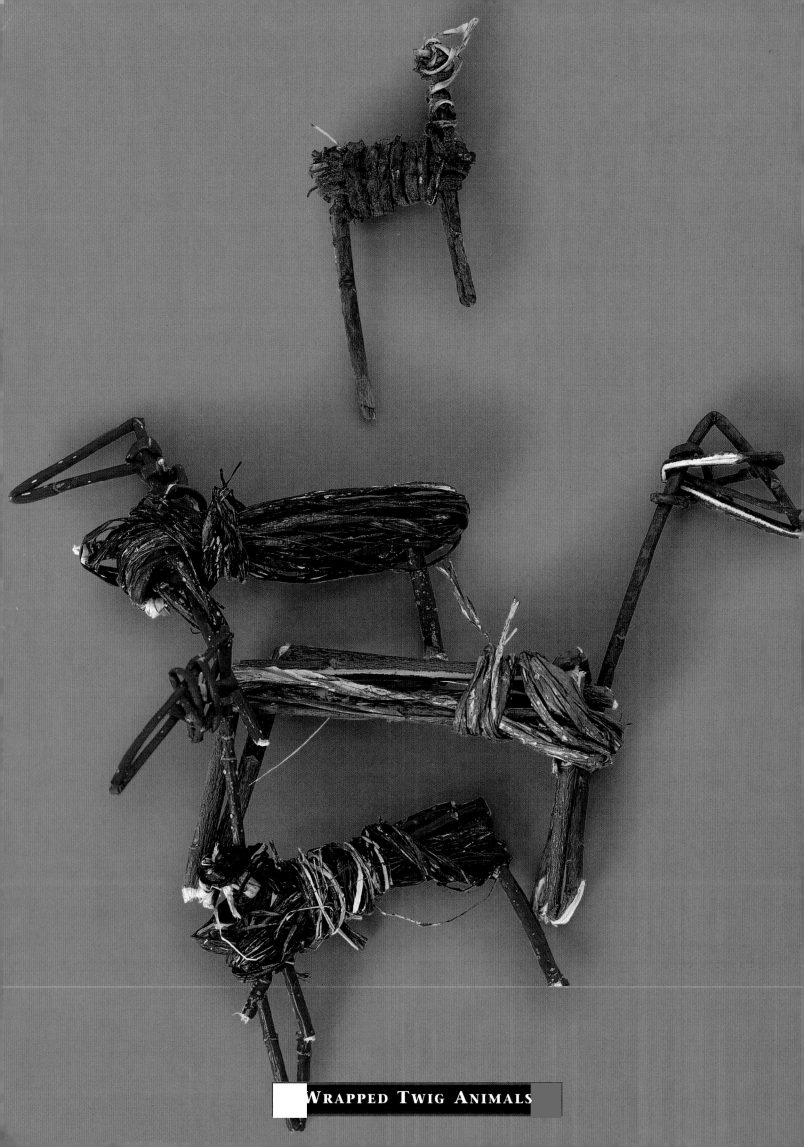

WRAPPED TWIG ANIMALS

WRAPPED TWIG ANIMALS

Materials: long, flexible, freshly picked twigs such as willow; optional thread for tying ends; and raffia for wrapping the twig body.

1. Give your animal a triangular head. Leave extra length. Bend twigs gently or they will snap.

2. Wrap the extra length around the animal's head or neck and tuck under or tie with thread.

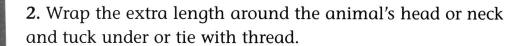

3. Bend twig for front legs, animal back, and back legs. If your twig is not long enough, tie on a second twig.

4. Wrap the rest of the twig back and forth around body. Tuck the end under or tie with thread.

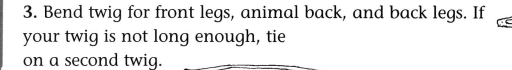

5. You may choose to wrap your twig animal with dark raffia strips. Two or three strips that are an arm's length will be enough.

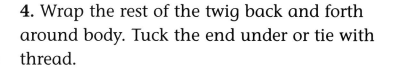

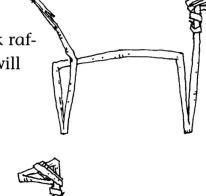

Long ago, in 6500 B.C., Archaic people in ancient desert caves such as Danger Cave in Utah, fashioned twigs into small animal figurines. Some think the figurines look like deer. Nobody knows why these people made split twig animals—perhaps they were toys or used for good luck in hunting.

Over 2,000 years ago the desert sands covered and protected the Archaic people's delicate twig animals, stone tools, mats, sandals, grinding stones, and rabbit snares. Today we can see these objects in museums and think about their use.

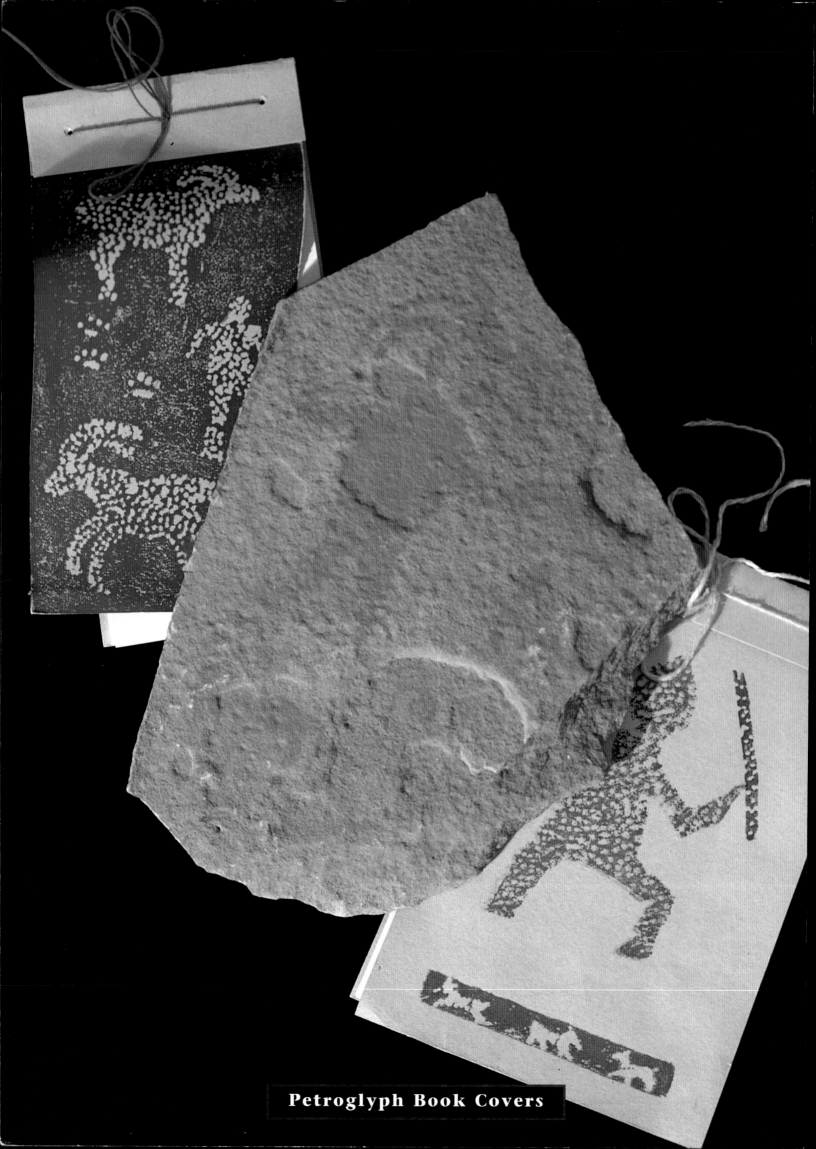

Petroglyph Book Covers

PETROGLYPH BOOK COVERS

Materials: a styrofoam meat tray without any design, a pencil, tempera paint, paintbrush or rubber roller, paper for book covers, paper for book pages, cord, paper punch, cookie sheet, and aluminum foil.

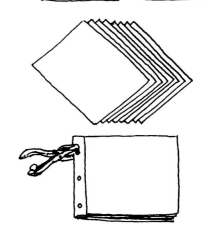

Preparing your Book
1. Choose book size and cut the front cover. Cut the back cover one inch longer than front. Fold the extra inch.

2. Cut book pages to match front cover size. Assemble back cover, pages, and front cover. Extend folded end over front cover. Punch three holes.

Making the Petroglyph Book Cover
1. Trim edges off the styrofoam meat tray. Using your pencil, peck a petroglyph design into the foam. See page 72 for ideas.

2. Use the paintbrush or roller to cover the cookie sheet with an even layer of paint. Quickly press foam printing plate face down into wet paint.

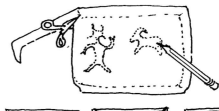

3. Lift foam plate from paint and press face down on book cover. Press firmly. You can turn it over so your cover is on top and continue pressing. Remove foam plate.

4. When the cover is dry, assemble the book. Tie covers onto the pages with cording. Direct the cord ends through the top and bottom holes to the back of the book. Bring both ends back through center hole and tie around front-facing cord.

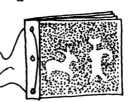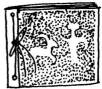

Anasazi and Fremont artists created pictures. Some of these pictures were painted on rock and called pictographs. Some were pecked into rock with hard tools. They were called petroglyphs.

ANASAZI WOVEN SANDALS

ANASAZI WOVEN SANDAL

Materials: each sandal requires one bag of natural raffia and one supple twig (for example willow or bridal wreath) about thirty inches long.

1. Measure your foot. Gently bend the twig and connect at heel base with raffia wrapping and knots.

2. Tie together 4 or 5 strands of raffia. Tie ends at heel and begin weaving over then under the side warps. Keep the woven rows snug. Continue up the sides of the sandal tying on additional strands of raffia. Keep ties as flat as possible and hidden on sandal "sole." When the sole is completed tie final strands at the top where toes will go.

3. To make "straps" tie on more raffia strands at heel, four or more for each side of foot. At a comfortable place on the instep, knot two "straps" together. Extend two parts to the top of sandal and tie at separate points on twig warp. Keep knots underneath. The straps go between the first and second toe.

The Anasazi relied on the yucca plant for many uses. The narrow-leaves of the yucca were used whole, or split, spun, or twisted into cordage. Yucca leaf sandals were a triumph of the Anasazi. They made many kinds of sandals using different weaving methods. Sometimes several techniques were used in a single pair. Sandal shapes varied from square heel and toe to scalloped toe and puckered heel to round heel and toe It took 450 feet of twisted yucca cordage to make a pair of tightly woven sandals. Modern TEVA® sandals are a derivation of the historic Anasazi creation.

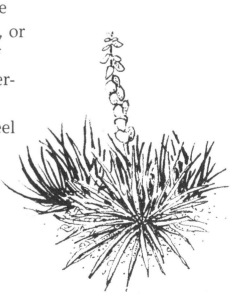

THE AMERICAN INDIAN

American Indians who managed the land and its resources for centuries in the Rocky Mountain region are recognized as distinct groups: each had a unique appearance and dressing style, often with identifiable patterns and colors; each had characteristic dwellings and village planning; and the stories, belief systems, and ceremonies of each group were highly specialized. Great care was taken to beautify the things they used and the clothing they wore. Shells, bone, teeth, quills from the porcupine and bird, and traded beads were sewn to clothing, headwear, and footwear.

THE LAND

In order to understand the cultures of the different American Indian tribes it is necessary to study the lands in which they lived; the land influenced everything from rituals to art to food supply. For example, the Gosiute Indians are thought of as "diggers," because their Utah land was dry and they dug for food, eating bulbs, roots, and animals that lived in holes such as snakes, gophers and other small rodents. The Red Rock Country Paiutes to the south are referred to as "gatherers" because they foraged for nuts and berries. Eventually they grew corn, melons, and wheat and used rabbit skins for clothing and blankets. Paiute women wove beautiful willow baskets. Seasonal weather, migrating animal herds, and irregular plant conditions kept most American Indians on the move. Some groups settled in lake or river valleys during seasons of the year. The eastern and southern areas of the West are desert climates with scant rainfall. The northern and central regions are covered with mountains, lakes, rivers, rich soil, and game.

THE PEOPLE

In the West, each tribe had several subgroups with distinct identities. Some common characteristics to all were:

- seasonal migration
- preservation of food
- design and production of containers
- hunting and food gathering groups
- agricultural abilities
- spiritual ritual and ceremony
- preparation of hides primarily for clothing and shelters

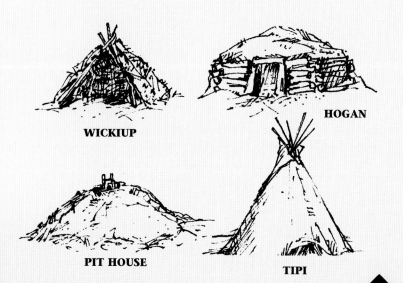

HOGAN

WICKIUP

PIT HOUSE

TIPI

THE DWELLINGS

The tribes made homes from the materials available in their surroundings. Several types of homes appear throughout the west. Conical tipis in varying styles were built in wooded areas. Stick, brush, and mud-formed wickiups were built by Gosiutes during the cold seasons. Navajos built six-sided hogans from clay and wood; and Paiutes built earth or sod homes.

THE HORSE

The western American Indian generally traveled by foot until the horse was introduced in the late 1500s. A Spanish horse dealer, Juan de Orate, brought
horses to America, then called "New Spain." By the 1650s the Ute
Indians were using horses as pack animals, but not yet riding them. By
1830 however, the Shoshoni and the Ute had become skilled riders and
their success as hunters and warriors rapidly increased. Elk, big horn
sheep, antelope, moose, rabbit, beaver, fox, and mule deer were harvested for
furs and hides, food, horns, hooves, and bone. The *travois*, a horse-drawn device
used to transport belongings, was invented to ease the nomadic lifestyle of the
American Indians.

THE PLANTS

American Indians used many plants for both nutritional and
medicinal purposes. The most widely used food plant was the
prairie turnip, called the Indian potato by trappers. It was gathered in the spring, grew to the size of a large avocado and was
eaten raw or in soup. This turnip could be sliced and sun dried to
store. The thistle and sego lily bulbs were also used for food; the
yarrow plant was used as salve for cuts and bruises; and sagebrush
was used to make yellow dyes.

ART AND SPIRITUALITY

American Indian art has profound spiritual significance and reflects a tribe's values. The Navajos
had a saying that the purpose of art is "to beautify the world." For the Navajo, beauty was perceived
as order in the natural and supernatural world. Even though each American Indian tribe had distinctive characteristics (they spoke over 50 different languages and existed independently of one
another) most tribes had a shaman or, spiritual leader. And, most tribes believed that humans, animals, and all of nature existed as one. Both giving and receiving were regarded as essential to main-
tain a sense of balance and well-being.

Among the tribes, there was a blending of art styles as a result of trading, fur swapping, gift
exchanges, war spoils, and intertribal marriages. Such interchange has made it difficult to properly
identify some artifacts.

   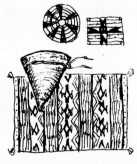 

*Author's Note: The term Native American was used throughout the writing and production of this book until the preview meeting with leaders
from the Indian community. They unanimously recommended the term ◆ become American Indian. We have complied with their request.*

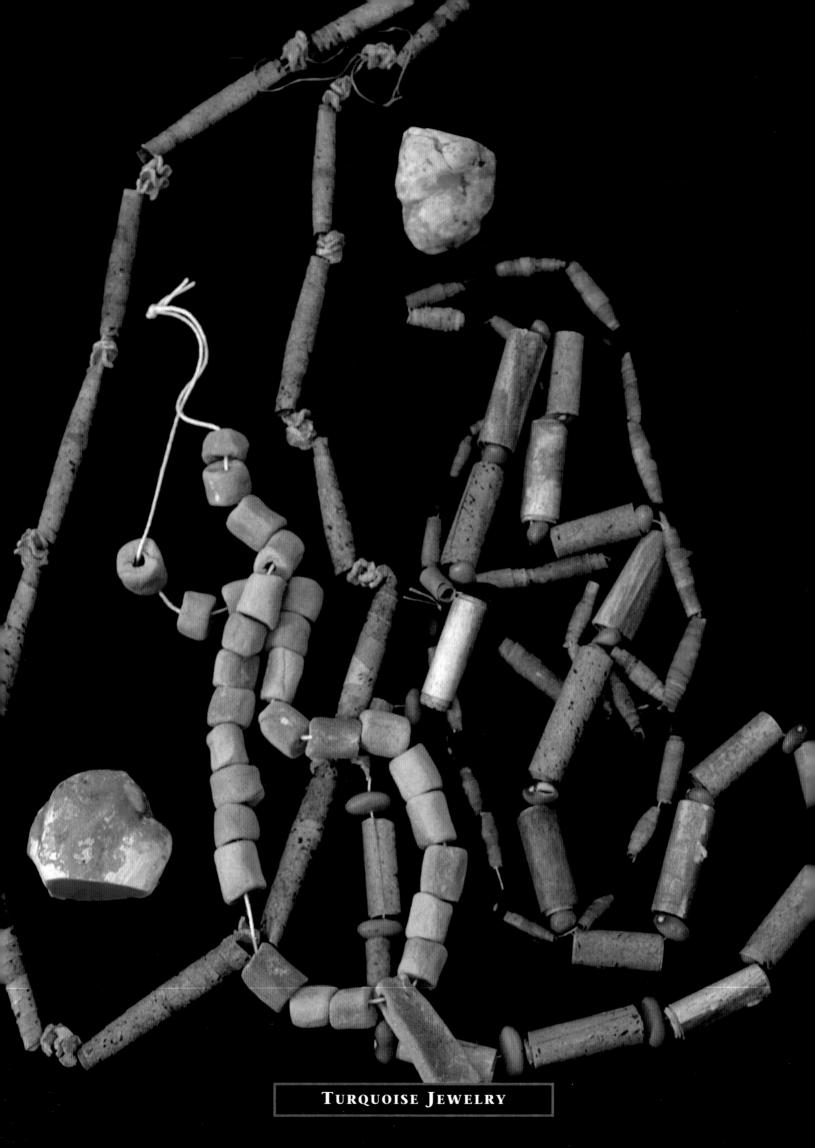

TURQUOISE JEWELRY

TURQUOISE JEWELRY

Materials: white butcher paper; acrylic or tempera paints in blue-green, yellow-brown, red-brown, and dark brown; a 2 to 3 inch foam brush (available at paint stores) or sponge; a toothbrush thin carrot circles;, soaked beans (black, pinto, or red chili work well—limas do not); an embroidery needle, dental floss, scissors, and white glue.

1. Making "turquoise" and "clay" beads:
   a. Creating "turquoise": apply blue-green paint to both sides of white paper with your brush or sponge. Small dabs of the other colors, heavily watered down, can be added to your sponge to mottle the "turquoise" color and give it an authentic look. *Spatter the paper.
   b. Creating "clay": apply red-brown paint to both sides of white paper using the same mottling technique as above. *Spatter the paper.
   *Spattering: use a dry toothbrush dipped in brown paint to flick dots on the painted papers. This is messy! Protect the surfaces around you or do it out-of-doors.

2. Forming the "turquoise beads": cut blue-green paper into 4 to 8 inch triangular strips. Roll-up strips starting from the wide-end. Insert a dab of glue when you reach the tip. For "clay beads" cut brown paper into 1 inch rectangular strips. Roll and glue.

3. Making jewelry: string beads with a needle and dental floss. Create interesting patterns with beans, carrots and your beads.

Southwest Indians venerated turquoise which symbolized the blue of water and the green of growing vegetation. There was a lively turquoise trade between pre-Hispanic Mexico and the Southwest tribes as desert turquoise had a rare and rich color.

TRANSITION DOLLS

A TRANSITION DOLL

Materials: one manila folder, scissors, glue, a hole punch, 4 brass brads, crayons, a pencil, scraps of colored paper, leather, etcetera.

1. Find the doll pattern on page 75. Trace doll pattern on the manila folder and cutout. Punch holes where indicated with the hole punch.

2. Attach the arms and legs at the joints with brass brads.

3. Next, dress the doll in paper, felt, or muslin "clothing." Because the doll is jointed, sleeves and trouser legs are cut double and attached separate from a "body" piece which extends from the neck and includes the entire torso.

   a. Cut 2 sets of blue pant legs and blue sleeves, and 1 set of the blue body piece for shirt and pants. Patterns for these are made by laying the body on the blue paper and tracing around it. Glue the double sleeves, pant legs, and body clothing to the doll. Make sure the joints can move.
   b. Cut the vest from a scrap of "leatherized" brown paper and tempera painted with designs. See page 74 for leatherizing technique.
   c. Cutout apron and decorate with crayons to match traditional beaded form.
   d. To create "chaps": paint paper, color with crayons. Attach with twine, thick thread, or floss.
   e. Paint the dentalium shell neck piece. Glue around neck.
   f. Use yarn to make hair and refer to page 76 for moccasin pattern.

The authentic doll pictured at left reveals the evolution of American Indian clothing from the contact period to the present day. Blue jeans are now worn by everyone. Yet, the handsome traditional over pieces are still retained and worn for certain occasions. Dentalium shells, a trade item from the Pacific Coast, are favored decorations even today.

LEATHER POUCH

A LEATHER POUCH

Materials: a large, brown paper grocery bag with folds cut and inside facing out; a piece of graph paper with 1/4 inch square; fine-tip markers in black, blue, red, green and yellow; a pencil, a ruler, scissors, a stapler, and glue.

1. The photographed pouch has been "leatherized". Refer to page 74 for leatherizing instructions. Leatherize before cutting the bag into pieces.

2. Cut a (A) 12 1/2 x 17 inch piece from the grocery bag. Cut a 6 1/2 x 2 inch strip from top leaving flap section. Make a peaked cut on flap.

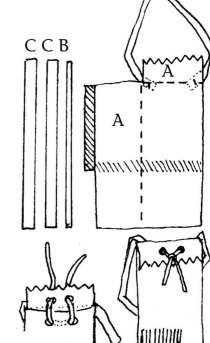

3. Cut one (B) 1/4 x 17 inch piece for the tie. Cut two (C) 1 x 17 inch strips to be joined for the long shoulder strap. Fold (A) on dotted lines. Staple strap to side of flap. Cut two holes in flap for tie. Make two matching holes on front of pouch. Glue pouch together. Apply glue to slash marked areas. Cut fringe 7 inches long.

4. For front panel, use a 5 inch square piece of graph paper. For side strips, use a 1/2 x 8 inch piece. To create a traditional appearance, color front panel in a geometric pattern. (Suggested colors in material section were used by the Ute tribe.)

5. Glue the "beaded" panel on the front of pouch above fringe. Fold narrow strips in half so 1/4 inch shows on front and back. Glue. Slip 1/4 x 17 inch tie through holes in front of pouch and out through holes in flap.

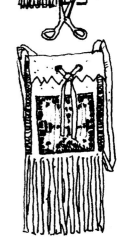

The Utes were hunter-gatherers who relied on containers. Ute pouches, similar to the bags we use today, were made for many uses. For instance, small bags were made for carrying domestic tools. Sectioned bags were made to hold pipe pieces and tobacco. And strike-a-light bags were constructed to hold fire-starting materials.

Animal bones, teeth and claws, shells, stones and quills were originally used to decorate the personal and ceremonial objects of the Utes and many tribes in the Rocky Mountain West. European traders introduced beads and by the late 1800s small glass seed beads had been adapted as important decorations.

ARM BAND

ARM BAND

Materials: a manila file folder, a piece of graph paper with 1/4 inch squares, a pencil, glue, scissors, fine-tip markers in red, green, blue, and yellow, leatherized paper (see page 74), 24 inches of colorful ribbon, 2 paper clips, masking tape, and a hole punch.

1. Measure the upper arm circumference of the person who will be wearing the arm band. The most common measurement is 10 x 3 inches. Cut from the folder. Cut out three sets of two circles: 1 1/2 inch, 1 inch, 1/2 inch. There should be six circles. Punch a hole in the middle of each circle so that the holes line up when the two sets are stacked, largest to the smallest.

2. Make a paper design that resembles the geometric patterns of beadwork. Look at the beadwork directory on page 72 for ideas. With a pencil and a piece of scrap graph paper make a rough sketch of your design.

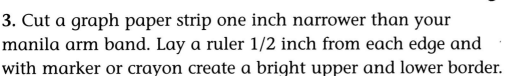

3. Cut a graph paper strip one inch narrower than your manila arm band. Lay a ruler 1/2 inch from each edge and with marker or crayon create a bright upper and lower border.

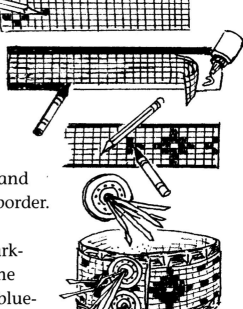

4. Make a bead pattern with pencil by counting and marking the pattern squares. After you have solidly colored the design, color in the background with white, yellow and blue-green which were commonly used. Now, color in your "beads."

5. Make the two rosettes by gluing the layered circles together. Poke your prepared cut strips of ribbon and leather through the hole. Punch four holes on each end of the arm band. Overlap and line the rosettes with the holes. Attach the strands with masking tape to the inside of the arm band.

Czechoslovakian glass beads, introduced by traders, became highly prized decorative items.

BALL IN THE CUP GAME

BALL IN THE CUP GAME

Materials: a 4 inch paper tube (toilet paper tubes work well), masking tape, brown shoe polish, yarn, colored paper strips, crayons or markers, string, thread or dental floss, one large bead, a large-eyed needle.

1. Cover your tube with torn, overlapping, masking tape pieces. Tape pieces over the edges of your tube. Cut out a 2 inch circle, insert, and glue in one end so there is only one tube end open.

2. Rub shoe polish or brown paint over the masking tape. Your tube should resemble wood, leather, or clay.

3. Look at the bead designs on page 72. Decorate a colorful band with a bead design and fasten around the middle of your tube.

4. String thread through a large-eyed needle and attach it to the rim of your tube. Pull the string through the large bead. Tie together the string ends. Now play the game with your friends. Can you get the ball into the cup on your first try?

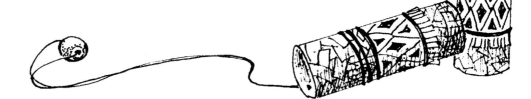

   Games and play, such as the cup and ball game, were an important American Indian tradition. Children often mimicked adult life in their games: little girls played with dolls, tiny tipis, and miniature cradleboards. Balls covered with leather and small bows and arrows were common play objects for boys.

STORY ROBE

A STORY ROBE

Materials: a piece of white butcher paper 36 x 36 inches; sponge for painting; acrylic or tempera paint in yellow, brown, and white; water in a container, markers or crayons, a pencil, and scissors.

1. Cut a section of butcher paper in the shape of a hide. ''Leatherize'' your paper (see page 74 for the technique).

2. Develop your concept and sketch on a piece of paper. Your story could be about your neighborhood, a sport you play or closely follow, your friends, your family, a pet, or an event in your life.

3. Draw your story lightly with pencil on the prepared paper. When you are ready, add color to your drawing. Ask a friend or family member if they can translate your picture story.

Story robes were produced in more than one form and for varying purposes. They always had two common characteristics: simple, painted figures used to reveal a story and figures painted on a prepared animal hide or, later, on canvas. Used to record and convey visions, the events of their calendar year, and tales of personal exploits, American Indian story robes were revered for their rugged beauty and unique character. Lewis and Clark collected several robes and sent them to President Jefferson.

A ROBE IS WORN TELLING OF A GREAT HUNT

A HIDE IS DISPLAYED TELLING OF A VICTORY

A TIPI TELLS A HISTORY OF THE FAMILY

STICK RATTLE

STICK RATTLE

Materials: several colors of yarn (each piece should be 2 to 3 yards long); a large-eyed needle; 8 inches of pliable wire; an 18 inch forked stick; buttons, colored beads, feathers, metal bells and bones (optional).

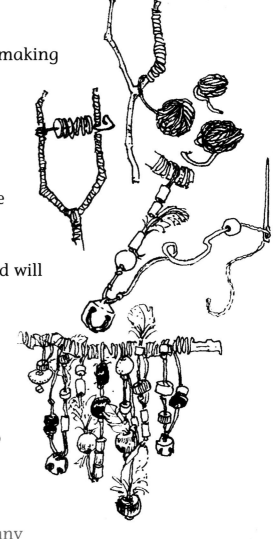

1. Wrap the forked stick with several pieces of yarn, making sure the yarn covers the bark.

2. Thread the buttons or drilled bones onto the wire. Securely wrap the wire around each fork end.

3. Put 10 to 12 inches of yarn through the needle eye and hide the end in the wrapped yarn at the end of the stick you hold.

   a. String a bead, then tie a large knot so the bead will not slip down.

   b. Pull string through the metal bell and turn your yarn to double it back to the stick base.

   c. String more beads on the return piece.

d. Glue in a few feathers as you go.

4. Extend the jangles of beads, bells, and feathers up the stem as far as you wish.

Rattles, drums, and rubbing sticks were used by many American Indians for ceremonies and rituals. Original stick rattles used drilled shells instead of buttons, bones and beads.

NAVAJO WOVEN BAG

NAVAJO WOVEN BAG

Materials: a 3 x 3 1/2 inch section of stiff cardboard; strong cotton for warp (weft yarn is made from the odds and ends of red, white, navy blue, and black); a pencil, a ruler, scissors, a large-eyed needle for the weft yarn, comb or fork to "beat down" the weft.

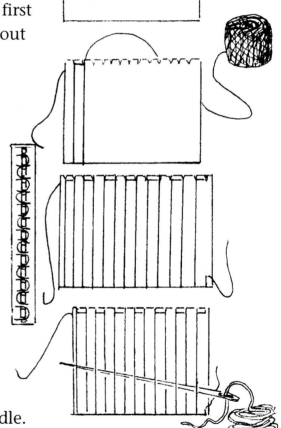

To weave a bag on a simple cardboard loom:
1. Choose which end of your bag will be open. At open end make marks for slots 1/4 inch apart except at corners where slots should be 1/8 inch apart. Cut slots 1/8 inch deep.

2. Warp your loom by securing the warp yarn in the first notch (it should wedge firmly in the notch), leave about 4 inches of extra warp.

3. Wrap warp thread down one side and around the bottom and back to the first notch and then back and around the second. Keep your warp thread tight.

4. Continue wrapping the warp yarn around the bottom of the loom into the second notch and back through the third. Finish the warping. **Never go over the top of the loom.** This is your bag opening. End by cutting a small slot at the bottom and wedge end of warp thread. Cut. Follow the diagram.

Planning and weaving your striped bag:
1. Begin weaving the weft at the bottom. Cut a piece of weft yarn as long as your arm and thread the needle. Go under the first warp over the second, under the third and over the fourth. You are weaving!

2. Repeat the pattern across the first side of your bag and pull weft through. Do not pull weft tight because a tight weft will pull in the sides of the bag. Beat down the weft with a fork or comb.

Continued on page 78.

37

THE TRAPPER

The trapper of the fur rendezvous era traveled by horse and mule throughout the Rocky Mountains in search of valuable beavers and other fur-bearing animals. Also called mountain men, trappers carried nearly all their necessities. Some items filled the "possible bag." Other objects were strung on heavy cord and worn around the neck or attached to a belt. Even saddlebags bulged with important commodities that had been carefully made or traded.

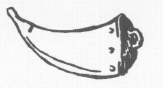  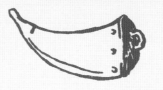

For many years trappers valued the West as a rich source of beaver, mink, otter, and marten skins. French trappers built forts, traded pelts, and mingled with Indian tribes during the 1600s and 1700s. At its peak from 1811 to 1840, trapping was the primary draw to the West. It wasn't until the Lewis and Clark expedition of 1803 that information concerning plants, animals, terrain, and the indigenous cultures was collected and documented.

Known as mountain men, trappers traveled throughout the west, usually following American Indian trails and documenting them on the West's first maps. Their travel on these trails contributed to the end of the American Indian's isolation. When the trapping era ended, trappers, regarded as an important source of knowledge, became guides for prospectors or wagon trains and ran trading posts.

The Beaver

The castoreum holds the castor gland for bait.

The trap and bait pan was laid underwater.

The trapper skins and scrapes the inside of the dead beaver.

The pelts are baled and stored to be sold at the rendezvous.

The hide was greased, tanned and stretched for drying.

THE BEAVER

The castor canadensis (beaver) is a rodent whose glossy, waterproof underfur has a natural tendency to mat or "felt," making it an ideal material for hats. The tan to dark brown fur was prized throughout Europe and beaver hats were the ultimate fashion statement for men for over two centuries. The value of other furs was determined by comparison to beaver fur.

Trapping the beaver and preparing the pelt was labor intensive and time consuming. First the trap was laid underwater where the beaver was caught and drowned. Then, the body was retrieved and skinned and the hide scraped. The hide was then greased, tanned, and stretched to dry. Finally, the pelts were baled and stored (cached) to be sold at the next fur rendezvous.

Trappers were only interested in the beaver's full, cold weather pelt. Prime trapping seasons were November until the freeze-up and March through April.

THE FUR RENDEZVOUS

The first fur rendezvous was in 1825 in the Flaming Gorge area of Utah and Wyoming. Six to seven hundred trappers were in attendance for this first gathering. Later rendezvous attracted several thousand trappers. These gatherings were times for story-telling, games of skill, gambling, and fur-selling. James

Beckwourth describes a rendezvous as, "a time of mirth, songs, dancing, shooting, trading, racing, jumping, yarns and frolic." But it was also a time for a trapper to reap the profits of many months of trapping. An exceptional trapper would present 600 to 800 pelts. The going rate for a pelt was $2.00. A fine beaver hat might then be sold in New York City for $10.00. A typical rendezvous lasted a month and most trappers made approximately $1,000 from fur sales.

PERS

THE MOUNTAIN MAN

The mountain man was nomadic, carrying with him all he needed to endure both cold and hot seasons; to find and prepare food; and to trap the animals by which he earned his livelihood. He wore buckskin pants, a cloth shirt, and various styles of headgear, all of which were designed to accommodate the change of seasons. He carried a little coffee, tea, flour, salt and sugar, but depended largely on the land, eating the lean meat he trapped, plus berries, roots, and herbs. Next to his gun and several different knives his most important survival tools were the six to eight traps he carried. To survive in the West, the trapper had to anticipate every need. The items he carried were practical, sturdy and precise in their design for portability and use. He carried a "possible bag," meaning it carried everything he could possibly need. The contents usually included:

1. A strike-a-light box used to start a fire including: flint, steel, and charred cloth patches.

2. A toothbrush made from carved bone and pig bristle plus a bag of baking soda.

3. A hinged, folding metal spoon or carved horn spoon

4. Bottles filled with sugar and salt

5. Candles

6. Horn buttons, metal needles, and an awl for hole punching.

7. Sinew for thread

8. Tobacco for personal use or trade

9. Bullets

10. Jerky to eat on the trail

11. The final item in the bag was a castoreum: a hollow wooden tube, tightly plugged, which held the castor gland of a beaver. The beaver's castor gland emits a strong scent designed to attract a mate. The trappers used it on beaver traps as bait.

SOME WELL-KNOWN TRAPPERS

Jim Bridger answered a newspaper ad and joined the Ashley-Henry Rocky Mountain Fur Company which started the Fur Rendezvous. He discovered the Great Salt Lake and built the emigrant way-station at Fort Bridger.

Etienne Provost, the namesake for Provo, Utah, was an experienced trapper in the Utah Lake and Green River region.

Jedediah Smith discovered South Pass, the Continental Divide and was the first to blaze a trail from Utah to California and on to the Pacific Ocean.

James Beckwourth, a famous African American trapper, kept one of the few diaries of this legendary era. He documented the 1826 rendezvous; trapped for Ashley's Rocky Mountain Fur Company; was both a guide and an explorer; fought in the Mexican war; and participated in the California Gold Rush. He lived his final years with the Crow Indians who named him "Buffalo Head" because of his thick, dark hair.

Peter Skene Ogden was a lawyer in Quebec, Canada when he joined the Hudson Bay Fur Company. His maps were the first reliable accounts of the northern Great Salt Lake and Nevada's Humboldt River. He trapped in Weber, Utah and explored the mountains behind his namesake, Ogden, Utah.

Miles Goodyear followed the mythical accounts of the exploration of the west as he grew up in Connecticut. He attended a fur rendezvous in 1832 and met Jim Bridger. He built Fort Buenaventura in Ogden, Utah on the Weber river, which is preserved and visited today as an historical site.

POWDER HORN

TRAPPERS

A POWDER HORN

Materials: one 2 ounce package of Sculpey™; a 5 x 5 1/2 inch section of poster board; a 1/2 x 36 inch strip of leather lace, felt, or similar material; a rolling pin or can; a table knife; a craft stick or other similar tool; tempera or acrylic paint in black, white and brown; an oven for low temperature baking, and scissors.

1. Cutout a powder horn wedge from the poster board (see wedge pattern on page 79). Soften the Sculpey™ in your hands. Reserve a walnut-sized ball for the powder horn lid.

2. Flatten the remaining Sculpey™ with your roller to a thickness of 1/8 to 1/4 inch. Lay Sculpey™ underneath wedge pattern and smooth with a roller.

3. Tape pattern together. Overlap at dotted line and use this as the form for wrapping Sculpey™ wedge. Join the two ends with your fingers. Keep the paper cone loose so it can be removed without sticking to the Sculpey™.

4. Form a ball at the tip of the horn for the shoulder strap attachment (1). Form the large end into a convex shape (2). Make a 1 1/2 inch "worm" which will be the loop to hold the shoulder strap or insert a paper clip 2/3 in (3).

5. Poke a hole in the center of the large end with a pencil. Gently press tips of loop into hole.

6. Make score marks around your powder horn with a table knife to indicate horn sections. On an actual powder horn this section is the removable tip allowing the gunpowder to be poured out.

7. Remove the paper cone form. Carefully attach the shoulder strap to the large, rounded end of the Sculpey™ cone. Gently curve the smaller end of the powder horn. Bake 10 to 15 minutes at 275 degrees.

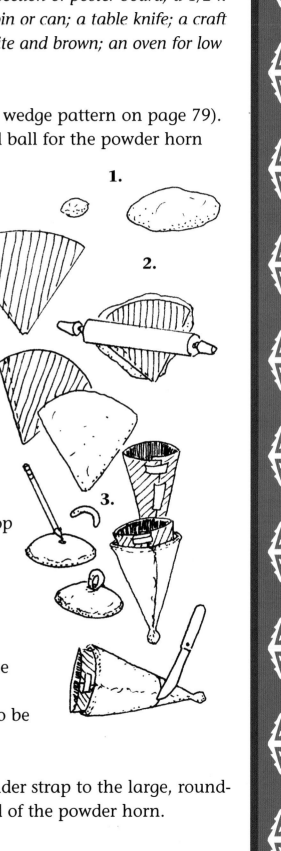

Continued on page 79.

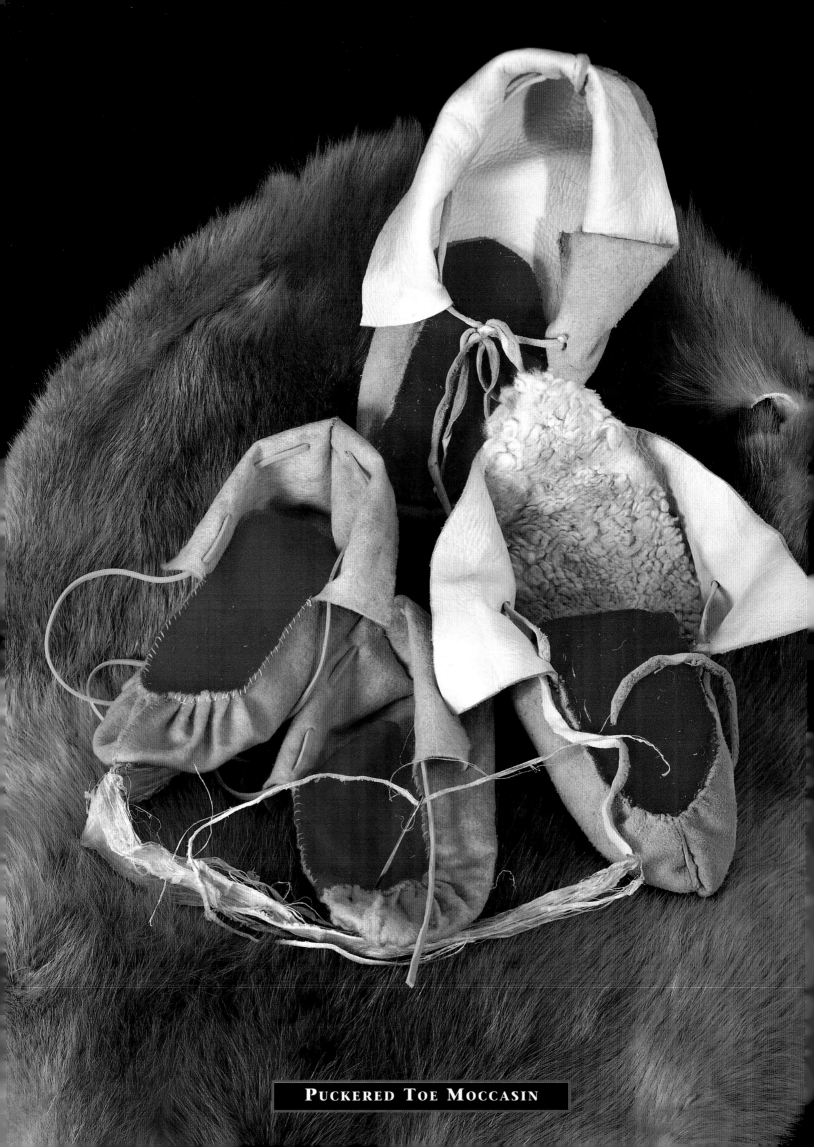

PUCKERED TOE MOCCASIN

A Puckered Toe Moccasin

Materials: two 11 x 12 inch pieces of buckskin-colored felt; two 3 1/2 x 6 inch pieces of red felt; heavy white thread or dental floss; two rawhide boot laces; scissors, a large-eyed needle, a paper punch (optional), and the pattern on page 76.

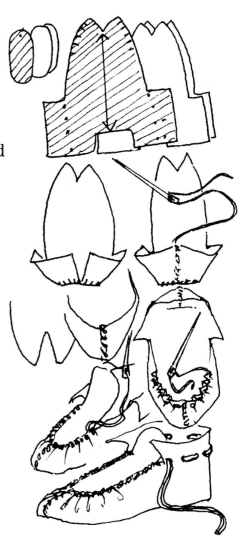

1. Size moccasin pattern by measuring foot from the back of the heel to the notch of the toe. Adjust length if necessary. Place pattern with dotted line on fold.

2. Cutout two tan and two red moccasin parts from the pattern. Cut a piece of dental floss as long as your arm and thread a needle. Knot the ends.

3. Using a whip stitch sew down each half of heel. Save enough for back seam to overlap 1/8 inch. Sew up back. Tie off seam by going over last stitch three times.

4. With knotted dental floss start at 'V' of toe and whip-stitch front toe seam.

5. Start at the center to pucker the toe, stitching down five pleats on each side of toe seam.

6. Find the center dot of the red insert piece. Match the center to the front toe seam. Stitch from center to flap. Tie off seam. Repeat on other side by starting at center and sewing to opposite flap. Tie off seam.

7. With a paper punch or tip of scissors cut small holes at dots. Lace your slipper.

After long days of setting beaver traps in cold mountain streams, a trapper looked forward to the comfort of his puckered toe moccasins. The moccasins were sewn with sinew, linen, or silk thread. The red insert was made from tightly woven wool cloth acquired from traders. The moccasins were all-weather footwear. The woolly insert made them warm in winter and unlined moccasins were comfortable for summer wear. The style was borrowed from the American Indian tradition and, in keeping with that influence, moccasins were often decorated with porcupine quills or seed beads.

KNIFE SHEATH

TRAPPERS

A KNIFE SHEATH

Materials: a 15 x 12 inch strip of poster board, a manila folder, tempera or acrylic paint in white, brown, and gray. Markers of intense colors in blue, red, and silver(optional), white glue, scissors, a stapler. Optional items are a large-eyed needle and coarse thread that will resemble sinew such as dental floss.

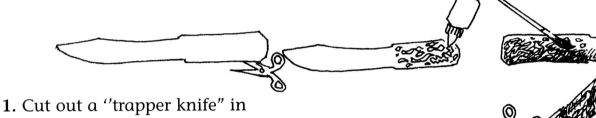

1. Cut out a "trapper knife" in one piece from the posterboard. Mark 6 inches for the handle and the rest for the blade. Texturize your knife handle to resemble bone using runs of glue. After the glue has dried (overnight), paint the handle with brown and yellow. Paint the knife blade gray or silver.

2. Make the leather-like cover for your knife sheath by laying the knife over a manila folder. Draw around the knife shape allowing a 1/2 inch margin on sides and bottom.

3. Making the fringe: Cut two long strips (about 15 inches each) from the manila folder. It should fit the bottom curve of sheath. Cut the narrowest fringe you can stopping 1/2 inch from the top. Sandwich the fringe between the paper sheath curved edges and staple.

4. Sponge or brush paint the sheath and fringe with brown and white paint in an uneven, tanned leather look. After it has dried, add the blue and red bead decoration with your marker. Attach the shoulder strap or belt loop.

A trapper's sheath was the ideal covering for his essential knife. A sheath fit only one knife. After the sheath was sewn it was dampened and the knife inserted so the leather dried to fit the knife's form. Trappers and American Indians bought the steel blades at the annual rendezvous. The handle for the blade was made from bone, wood or antler.

Note: If your program has a "weapons facsimile" policy, make only a few knife sheaths and display them. Do not allow them to leave your space with students.

HANDSOME HATBAND

TRAPPERS

A HANDSOME HATBAND

Materials: graph paper cut in 1/2 inch, 1 inch or 2 inch strips depending on your preference; coloring materials such as markers, crayons, or colored pencils; a lead pencil, and scissors. Feathers and beads are optional.

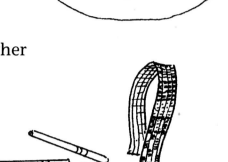

1. Look at the bead and quill patterns on the directory page 72. Choose a pattern for your hatband.

2. Measure the base of your hat. Cut enough graph paper strips to match hat circumference. Glue ends together to form a single long piece and attach.

3. Cut a piece of graph paper for your trial pattern design and fill in the squares with dark and light pencil. When ready, apply colors to the squares of your cut graph paper.

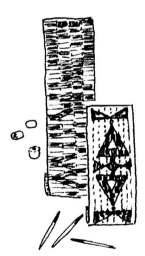

4. You now have a paper variation of a quilled or beaded hat band. You may wish to further decorate it with feathers and beads.

Porcupine quills were widely used as accents before traders introduced glass beads, yarns, fabrics, and braid. In turn, trappers learned quilling from American Indian women.

In the Cheyenne tribe, a woman's achievements in the decorative crafts were valued as highly as a man's deeds in war. A woman described the objects she had adorned as proudly as a man recited his deeds of battle. Women of special accomplishment formed associations. One such exclusive group, the Quiller Society ceremoniously performed the sacred task of decorating leather with distinguished porcupine or bird quills.

Approximately three to four inches in length, porcupine quills are white with brown tips. The women first sorted the quills, then dyed and softened them. They were then flattened with a fingernail or a piece of bone and sewn onto a leather surface with a needle and sinew thread.

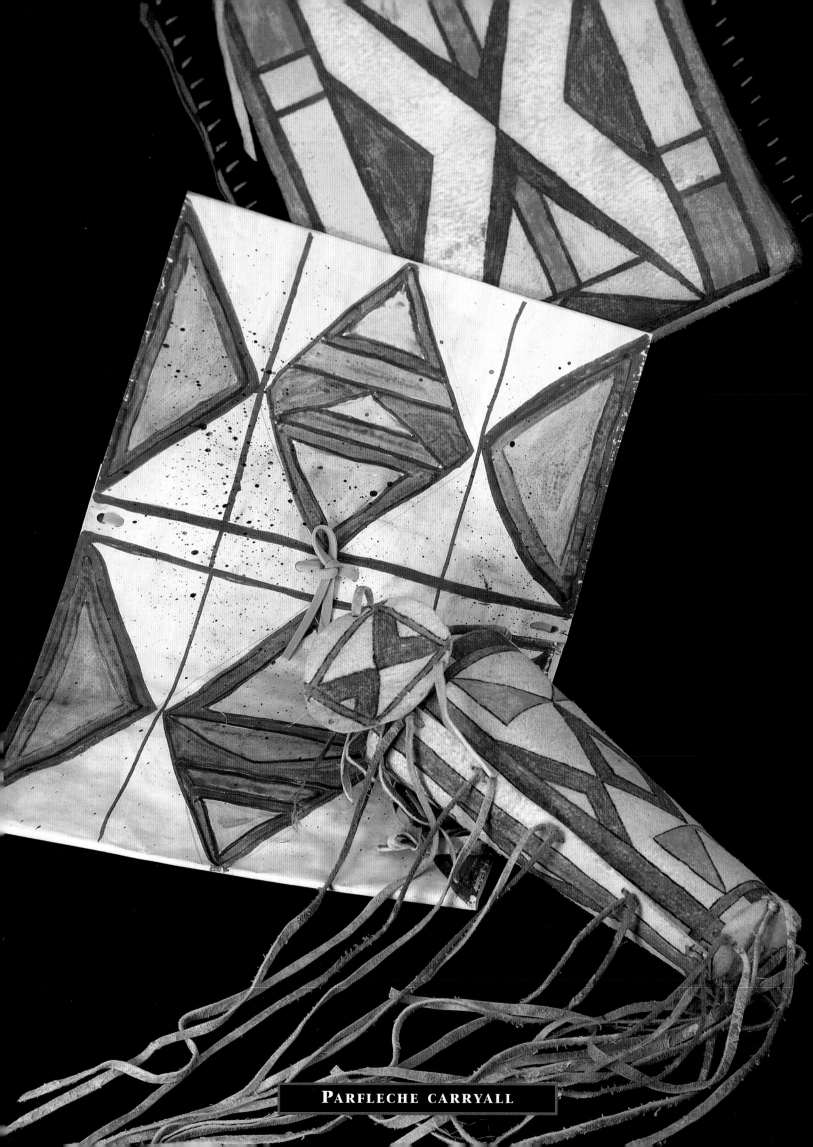

Parfleche carryall

A PARFLECHE CARRYALL

Materials: an 18 x 36 inch piece of white butcher paper; tempera or acrylic watercolor paints in light brown, red, blue, yellow, and green; a paintbrush, a toothbrush, scissors, a pencil, a paper punch, a blue wide-tipped marker, 1/4 x 36 inch piece of leather-like material for the tie, a sponge and paper plate, and a container of water.

1. See Leatherizing Paper instructions on page 74.

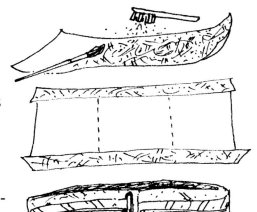

2. When your prepared paper is dry, fold in the top and bottom edges 6 inches. Next, fold paper into thirds with left side overlapping right side by one inch. You now have a basic parfleche carryall.

3. The parfleche was almost always decorated with geo-metric designs in red, blue, yellow, and green. With a pencil, sketch a design on the unfolded side of the parfleche. The design should be a mirror-image top to bottom and side to side.

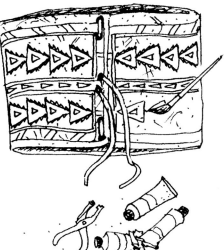

4. Paint your parfleche with the four traditional colors. Use a wide-tipped blue marker to outline shapes.

5. Punch two holes 1/2 inch apart on each end and in the center. Punch matching holes on the other side. Pull ties through the holes and join at center, firmly tie to keep your carryall from losing its cargo.

  Parfleche is a French word meaning "to deflect weapons." This ingenious, rectangular, flat envelope of rawhide was used to transport items such as dried meats and clothing. The trapper adopted the handsome *parfleche* design from the American Indian and the trapper's wife designed and painted the exterior according to traditional American Indian aesthetics. The handsome envelopes were used as saddlebags, strike-a-light containers, and hardy all-purpose luggage.

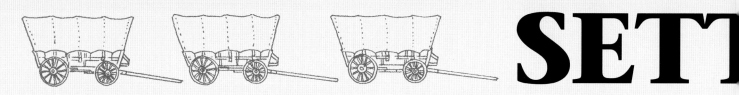

With the now famous phrase: "Go west, young man!' 'the westward movement commenced in the early 1840s. A steady stream of men, women, and children packed their essential belongings and left Independence, Missouri in covered wagons. From a distance the long wagon line resembled a flotilla of boats and the wagons were soon nicknamed "prairie schooners." The four to six month journey cost a family from $700 to $1500 dollars with most members walking part of the 2,000 mile trek. The travelers were trappers, missionaries, European emigrants, and Americans searching for religious freedom or the fertile paradise promised by promoters and the government.

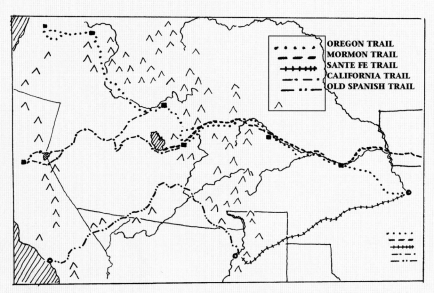

OREGON TRAIL
MORMON TRAIL
SANTE FE TRAIL
CALIFORNIA TRAIL
OLD SPANISH TRAIL

THE TRAILS

Settlers followed many different trails on their westward move. Beginning in Independence, Missouri and ending at Fort Vancouver, Washington, the Oregon Trail was the main westward route. This trail paralleled much of the Mormon Trail, which also began at Independence but ended at the Great Salt Lake. A third route, the California Trail, turned south to Sacramento. From Sacramento, the Old Spanish Trail extended to Los Angeles. Yet another famous route, the Santa Fe Trail, started in Independence and ended in Santa Fe, New Mexico. Though the traveler had several trail options, no route avoided the forbidding mountains, pitiless deserts, and Indians. The Great Basin of Utah and Nevada was an especially treacherous part of the trail. Here settlers faced 200,000 square miles of white, salty sand, baked clay, and the intense reflection off the Great Salt Lake. A California bound woman wrote, "I have suffered more this afternoon than all my sufferings put together." Once through the Rocky Mountains and South Pass, the Oregon settlers separated from the Utah and California bound groups.

THE OXEN

Oxen were used to move settlers westward. Less expensive and easier to train than horses, oxen also adjusted more easily to extreme temperatures; were less likely to be stolen; and were less susceptible to disease. An oxen, with hooves shod for better traction, could steadily pull a heavy load over rough ground during the journey as well as till the ground and haul lumber, stone, and rock once the destination was reached. Linked in two to three teams per wagon, they covered an average of twelve miles a day.

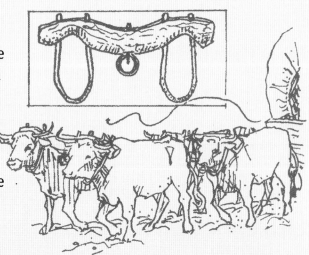

LERS

THE LOADING OF THE COVERED WAGON:

Covered wagons could move 1,000 pounds of food, cooking utensils, bedding, clothing, weapons, and tools over the western terrain. The wheels were removable and the canvas was waterproofed with linseed oil for river crossings. Selecting, weighing, and loading provisions impacted a family's ability to survive during the crossing. Only a few cherished family albums, china pieces, or furniture items could accompany the family to their new home.

Trouble with American Indians was rare and trading usually consisted of a peaceable exchange of clothing, ironware, and furnishings for buffalo meat and food staples. Accidents and disease were more common traveling hazards. One out of seventeen travelers, or about six percent, died on the trail, with cholera the most common cause of death. Accidental gun shot wounds took their toll.

CROSSING RIVERS

BUFFALO STAMPEDES

CLIMBING MOUNTAINS

REPAIRING WAGONS

THE PIONEER HOME

Even after the settlers reached their final destination, the covered wagon continued to provide shelter. Temporary tents helped with overflow, but often months passed before a crude dug-out home was ready for wintering. If timber was scarce, clay bricks, or sod cuttings were used to fashion make-shift homes. Often several years would pass before timber cabins were built. But by the turn of the century, fine Victorian homes and mansions dotted the frontier.

TENT

DAILY LIFE ON THE FRONTIER

The settlers learned to improvise. Soap was made from lye and fat; dye was made from bark and plants; tea was brewed from sage and salves from yarrow root; carrots and boiled sugar were combined and made jam; eyewash was made from gunpowder dissolved in water; onions mashed in sugar became cough syrup; and goose grease and turpentine were used as a poultice for the chest during a cold. A Spokane, Washington settler wrote to his friends in Maine detailing daily chores: "digging wells, herding livestock, gardening, making shoes, butchering meat, dipping candles, making soap, baking bread, washing clothes, sewing, milking cows, and raising children."

SOD HOME

LOG HOME

A pioneer wrote about the early times in Oregon country, "I never saw so fine a population as in Oregon. They were honest, because there was nothing to steal; sober, because there was no liquor; there were no misers because there was no money; and industrious because it was work or starve." The settlers were naive about the trials presented by "going west." Nonetheless, they faced each obstacle with determined heroism and ultimately succeeded in the new frontier.

For more about settlers, see **Hands-on Pioneers,** published by Deseret Book.
SLC, Utah. 1995. ISBN #1-57345-0855.

STANDARD HOME

Rag Rug

THE RAG RUG

*Materials: a piece of stiff cardboard for a loom (6 x 6 inches is a good starter size),
11 1/2 yards of strong cotton thread, patterned cotton scraps, scissors for cutting cloth,
a ruler, a pencil, and a fork to "beat down" the rug weft.*

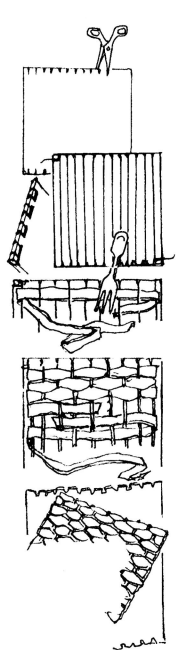

1. Prepare rags by cutting one inch strips. Use several complementary colors: red and green, blue and orange, yellow and purple.

2. Make a "loom" with your piece of cardboard. Make marks for slots 1/2 inch apart on edges of board. Cut slots 1/8 inch deep.

3. Warp the loom by securely tying warp string around first slot. Continue wrapping warp string up and down and around top and bottom slots. Finish by tying warp around last slot.

4. Begin weaving your rug. Start with a rag strip as long as your arm. Weave end backwards over and under to secure strip then weave over and under across the loom. Fold. Tuck edges under so woven strip has a neat appearance. Beat down woven strip with a fork.

5. Continue weaving until you run out of the color or wish to change color. To add a new strip overlap 3 or 4 warp threads with the new rag strip. Continue weaving and beating. Your rug is finished when no more folded strips can be woven in. Tuck the last end underneath.

6. Fold down slotted edges and slide rug off loom. Adjust weft so it is even.

Rag rugs, woven on large looms, were colorful, practical floor coverings. Women often gathered with friends to prepare rug rags. After cutting strips and sewing the ends, the rags would be rolled into a ball. The patterned fabric weft, woven into bright and sturdy warps, made a durable, welcoming carpet.

CATTLE BRAND QUILT

CATTLE BRAND QUILT

Materials: patterned quilting paper such as origami, gift wrap paper, or discarded wallpaper samples, a pencil, a ruler, scissors, dark tempera or acrylic paint, and glue, fabric paint in a tube. Refer to quilting ideas on page 72.

Note: our branding quilt was done as a four team cloth quilt with planned borders. These directions are for an individual quilt square.

1. Choose a quilt pattern from the suggestions on page 72. Enlarge the square to the desired size. The square must have some empty space for the brand (these traditional quilt squares do).

2. Cut a template for each different shape in your pattern. Carefully trace as many of each as you need. Cut out shapes. Exact measuring and cutting is necessary in order for shapes to fit together.

3. Assemble your quilt pieces on light or white backing paper. Glue in place.

5. To make and print the brand follow number 3, "Branding Prints" on page 65. After testing the brand on scrap paper print it on the quilt square in the white spaces or use fabric paint.

   Quilts are an American art form. To escape the loneliness of frontier life, women often gathered to form quilting bees. Quilts are then passed from generation to generation.
   In 1995, Edith Gentry, of Roosevelt, Utah introduced a novel addition to the tradition of quilt making. She used livestock brands that had been important to her as artistic symbols. Brands are the heraldry of the range--symbols of ownership, and an important figure of identity. We have adapted her idea as a variation on the traditional pieced quilt.

THE COWBOY

The early cowboy of the 1860 cattle drives relied on nearly the same gear as today's ranching buckaroo. Every cowboy paid special attention to his saddle, his lariat, and his clothing, especially his hat and boots.

There were several styles of such well-used articles and they were usually classified as "dressy" or "working." The working saddle was made of simple leather that molded to fit the rider's form. A comfortable fit—a priority in the cowboy's rugged world—was a necessity with boots, gloves, chaps, and hats. But, when the cowboy spruced up to "go to town" he glittered with a sizable silver buckle, a bolo tie, a silk scarf, a horse-hair braided hat band, and fancy spurs.

The great cowboy era lasted just 25 years, starting at the end of the Civil War and lasting until the mid 1880s. Known for their stamina in the face of physical hardship, cowboys were responsible for herding and tending to the welfare of cattle. For three to four months at a time, these people: Americans, African Americans, Mexicans, and European emigrants endured extremes of temperature and hazardous conditions for a mere $100. Records indicate that just forty thousand cowboys herded and drove over two million cattle to railroad pens or to the northern range alone.

To offset their challenging and often lonely existence, cowboys relied on books, ballads, and poetry. The cowboy is still considered a vital worker on western ranches and cowboy poetry has developed into a popular performance art. The nostalgic, humorous, and descriptive verses are composed and presented by the poet often with the accompaniment of campfire musicians and their harmonica, jew's harp and guitar.

THE VAQUERO

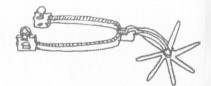

The first cowboys, the Spanish vaqueros, traversed the Mexico-California range 100 years before the advent of American cattle drives. Early Franciscan missionaries brought cattle to the range and they flourished on the rich California grass. The animals were val-ued for their hides and tallow (a fat used to make candles and soap). The Franciscan fathers trained their Indian converts to ride horses and herd the growing numbers of cattle. By the mid 1860s cattle were being sold for beef. The vaquero's high style and expert riding inspired much of the exotic image equated with today's cowboy. Many cowboy words have Spanish roots: *chaperreras* inspired "chaps," *la reata* is the origin of "lariat" and *vaca* (cow) evolved into "buckaroo."

A COWBOY'S EQUIPMENT

Spurs

The first thing a cowboy did with a new set of spurs was file down the points so they would not injure the horse. He rarely removed his spurs: they were an essential component of his image. The jingling metal created sweet music to the ears. Every cowboy had a pair of daily work spurs and some had a pair of dressy silver spurs for special occasions.

WORK SPURS   DRESS SPUR

The Cow Pony

The cow pony, or plains mongrel, was an important and much relied upon resource for the cowboy. The tough, half-wild animal was a combination of plains mustang and U.S. Cavalry thoroughbred. Cow ponies were six feet tall and weighed 700 pounds compared to today's western horses which typically stand 7 feet tall and weigh a thousand pounds. "Breaking" these four year old ponies took four to six days. The "breaker" was usually a specialist who traveled from ranch to ranch.

The Essential Lariat

The *reata,* or lariat, was the cowboy's primary tool. A typical forty foot lariat was made from expertly braided rawhide or twisted grass. Seldom out of the cowboy's hands, the lar-iat was used to rope calves for branding; restrain uncooperative horses or steers; reign in stray cows; or rescue bogged wagons.

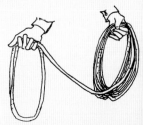

WBOY

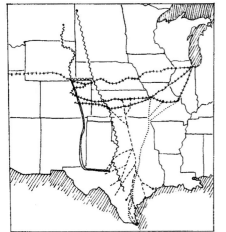

- ············· SHAWNEE
- -------- CHISOLM
- ∿∿∿∿∿ WESTERN
- ═══════ GOODNIGHT-LOVING
- ++++++++ RAILROAD

THE CATTLE DRIVE TRAIL

By 1876, the year of the nation's Centennial, the United States was divided into the populated East and the perceived barren, inhospitable West. Mark Twain said, "It is mighty regular out here in Nevada about not raining but as a general thing the climate is good, what there is of it." However, seven western states and nine territories were rich in grass and perfect for grazing cattle.

The main cattle trails for the long drives ran north from the longhorns' home breeding grounds in Texas. Here were trunk lines with branches spreading as far west as California and Oregon. The Shawnee trail heading northeast to Missouri was off limits due to a quarantine on the fever-bearing longhorns not to mention the Civil War. After the war, the beef business boomed as the railroad expanded and brought more settlers to the west. The Chisolm Trail, 400 feet wide in places, was the most accessible and thus most heavily traveled route.

BRANDING

Cowboys who could neither read or write could always recognize livestock brands. The brand, a symbol burned into the cattle's hide, was a sign of ownership and many ranches were named after the owner's brand. Branding has been practiced throughout history. Four thousand year old Egyptian tomb paintings show brands on cows and Cortés' cattle were marked with three crosses. Cortés also branded Indian slave herdsmen on the cheek with a 'G' for "guerra," meaning war.

COWBOY NAMES OF THE ERA

Nat Love, a rodeo celebrity, was born a Tennessee slave in 1854. As a trail cowboy, he drove cattle and handled horses. Butch Cassity was a young cowhand on the Two Bar Ranch in Wyoming in the 1880s. On special occasions guests were entertained by the marksmanship of this sharp shooter. Within a few years he became an outlaw legend. Theodore Roosevelt made the journey west at the age of twenty-five. He later bought a ranch and referred to this era as the moment when "the romance of my life began."

SILVER BUCKLE & WESTERN VEST

A Silver Belt Buckle

Materials: a smooth styrofoam meat tray large enough for 2 x 3 inch buckle; heavy-duty aluminum foil, scissors, a blunt pencil, a 24 x 1 1/4 inch sheet of tan craft foam, masking tape, 6 brass brads, and a stapler.

1. Cut a buckle base from the styrofoam. A standard size is 3 inches by 2 inches. Lay styrofoam buckle base on the foil. Cut foil 1/2 inch larger than the styrofoam.

2. Make a figure eight with a 12 x 3/8 inch foam strip. Staple together and attach to foam buckle back with two strips of masking tape.

3. Wrap foil smoothly over styrofoam. Press extra foil neatly toward back. Draw your buckle design on paper then carefully engrave your design on the foil with a pencil point.

4. Work 1 inch of foam belt through loops on both sides. Cut 1/8 inch slits for brads at intervals. To take off belt, remove one brad.

Western belts and buckles aren't just for holding up jeans: they are a personal statement. Buckles are often made of elaborately engraved silver; and, rodeo winners might receive a prize buckle as a trophy.

A Western Vest

Materials: an 18 x 36 inch section of butcher paper or the inside of a brown paper bag, a pencil, masking tape, a glue stick, scissors, odds and ends for decoration (brass brads, ribbons, buttons, beads, yarn etc.).

1. Vest wearers will be different sizes. Measure your front and back across and down and cutout a back section and two front sections of vest. Lay the three pieces flat. Glue pockets on lower halves of front sections. Decorate the front and back.

2. Next, glue front sections to back section at shoulders and sides. Reinforce inside seams with masking tape.

A cowboy or cowgirl often wore a vest because it provided extra warmth, extra pockets, and a chance to express personal style.

PRINTED CATTLE BRAND

PRINTING A CATTLE BRAND

Material: scarf fabric or paper for making gift wrap; a potato or soft foam such as the type used for foot care, a 3 inch square of stiff cardboard for attaching the print material; dark tempera or acrylic paint or water-based printing ink; a paintbrush or rubber roller; a smooth, glass-like printing surface (plexiglass is excellent); a pencil, and scissors.

1. Plan your brand design on paper.

2. With a safe knife (for the potato) or scissors (for the foam), cutout your brand. Mount the potato or foam brand on the cardboard.

3. With roll or paintbrush apply color evenly to the brand surface.

4. First, invert and stamp brand on scrap paper. Press evenly and firmly. When you are happy with the results, re-ink your stamp and print brand on scarf or paper surface.

A brand is a symbol of ownership that was burned on all livestock with a hot metal tool called a branding iron. As significant as a coat of arms, the brand legally belongs to a particular ranch. Brands were painted on ranch buildings, tooled into leather, and stamped in silver.

BOLO TIE

THE BOLO TIE

Materials: Sculpey™ molding and baking "clay," a small brush, modeling tools (craft sticks, toothpicks, etcetera), ribbon or cord for the tie, acrylic or tempera paint.

1. To make the bolo and the bolo loop, work the Sculpey™ to soften. Make a loop to keep the string or bandanna ends in place (a bandanna requires a larger loop).

2. Create the bolo from a large walnut-size ball of Sculpey™. Roll half of it flat, cut it, texturize it, and attach your sculpted clay symbol to the prepared circle. (Consider making your own brand such as an animal, your initial, etcetera).

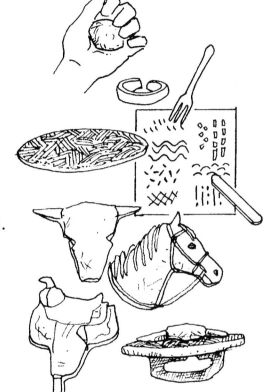

3. Attach bolo loop to back of bolo. Bake at 250 degrees for one hour. The bolo will harden as it cools. Paint with acrylic or tempera paint. Pull tie through the loop in back of the bolo. Tie a knot and secure.

 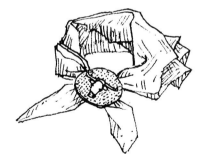

When cowboys or cowgirls dress up they often wear dress boots, silver dress spurs, and dress shirts. They may also wear a distinctive neck piece such as a bolo tie or silk scarf.

The bolo tie is a string-tie held in place by a piece of jewelry made from silver, a handsome stone, or even decorated leather.

BUCKAROO SPURS

BUCKAROO SPURS

Materials: half a sheet of black poster board; silver cardboard in the form of a 9 inch round cake plate (look in a party store); two gold notary stickers, a 12 inch black pipe cleaner, one plastic straw, 4 brass brads, 2 4 inch rubber bands, glue, scissors, a paper punch, two bells, and a pencil.

1. Cut three double parts from the black poster board of patterns #1, #3, and #5. Next, cut (from the silver cardboard) one double part of pattern #2 and four parts of #4. Glue #2 silver to #3 black. Decorate with notary seals.

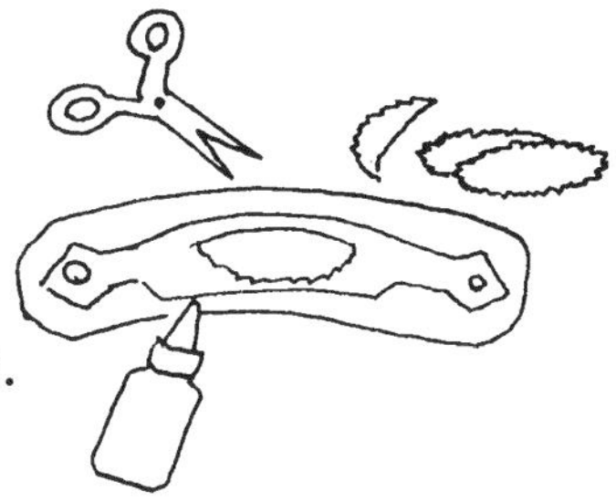

2. Punch holes at dots and cut slots on #5.

3. Connect #3A to #5A and #3B to #5B with brads.

4. Slip #1 through the slots in #5. Cut a 1/2 inch section of straw for each spur. Glue wheel so silver shows on both sides. Push wheel onto straw section. Thread pipe cleaner through straw, attach the bell and wrap around notches.

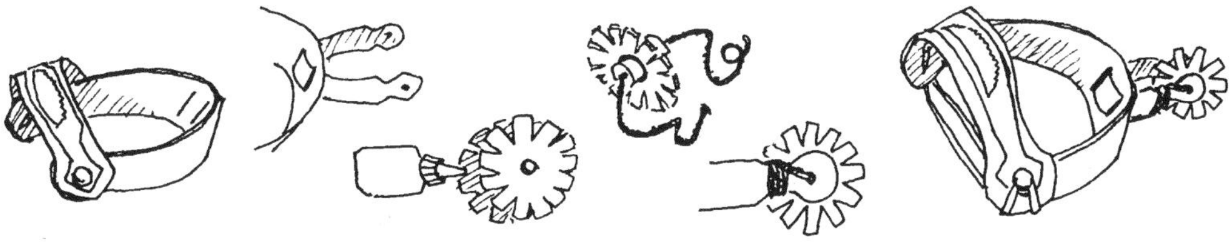

5. Catch rubber band around brads to fit under shoe instep. Thread pipe cleaner through straw and wrap around notches.

A o

#5

B o

#1

#2

#3

A o

B o

#4
add notches

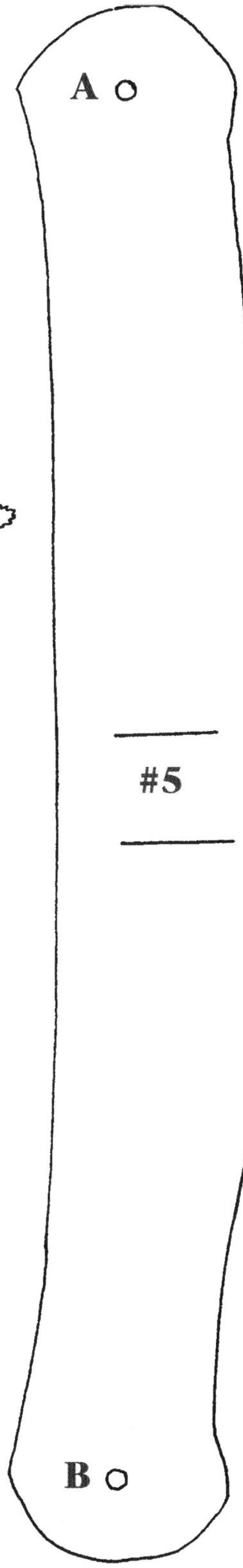

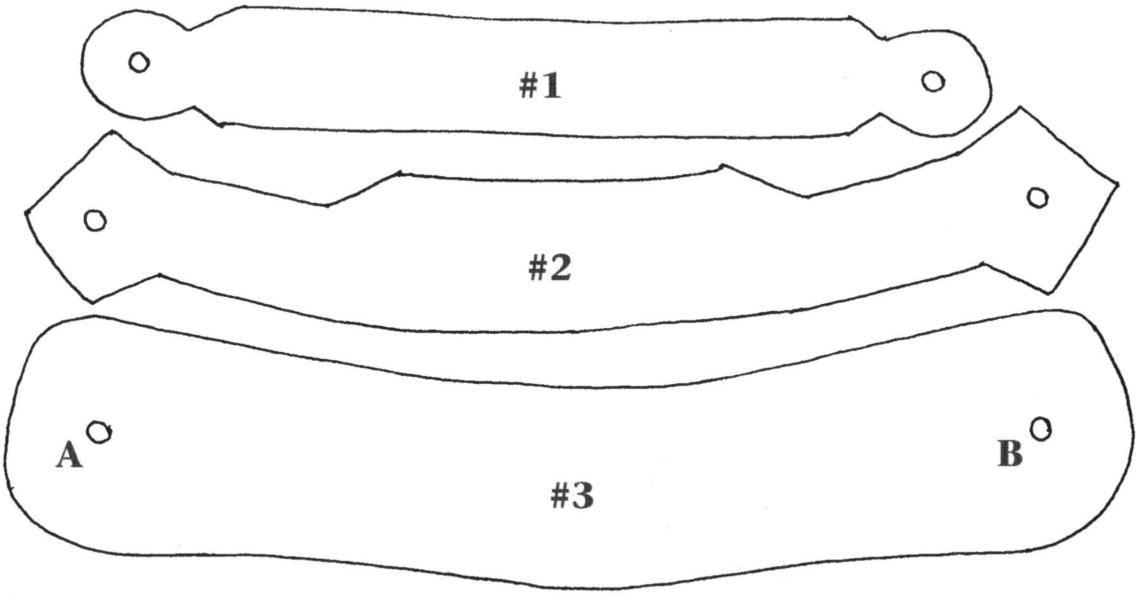

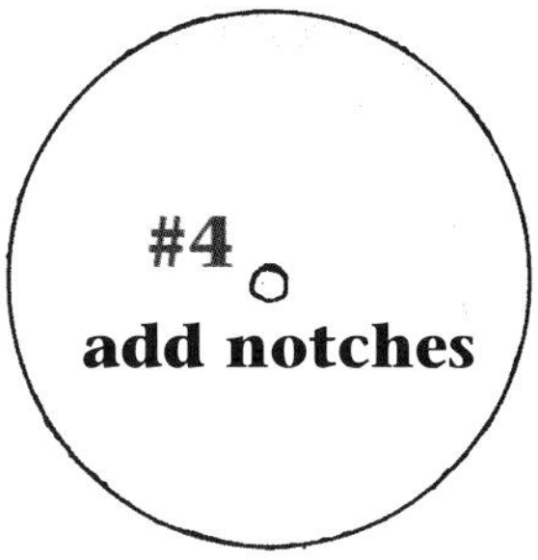

PAPER CHAINS

PAPER CHAINS

Materials: a large sheet of brightly colored paper (such as butcher paper, construction paper, wrapping paper, or wallpaper), scissors, a pencil, a sponge or rag, water-based paint, a tray for paint, glue or paint, patterns on page 77.

1. Cut the paper into strips as wide as desired and as long as possible.

2. Fold the strip accordion-style into 3 or 4 sections. Cut off any excess paper.

3. Choose a pattern from page 77.

4. With your pencil trace the pattern from our pattern pages or design your own. Make certain that some part of the design extends at least to the folded sides so that when it is cutout the shapes will be connected.

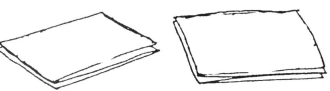

5. You may want to sponge paint your paper chain. Wait for paint to dry before cutting. To cut, fold the strip again and cut-out the shape you have drawn. To keep the layers of paper from sliding around while you cut, staple or paper clip the strips together on the part of your paper that will be cut away.

6. Repeat as desired until you have several strips. Fasten together the parts of your chain using glue or tape.

The paper chain motifs for the cowboy were inspired by the iron cutouts often seen above the gate to a ranch.

DIRECTORY
Design and Pattern Reference

ANASAZI PETROGLYPHS

ANASAZI POTTERY DESIGNS

AMERICAN INDIAN BEADWORK

FREMONT POTTERY DESIGNS

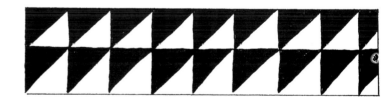

QUILT PATTERNS

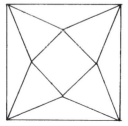 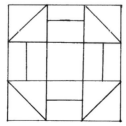 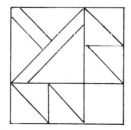 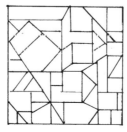 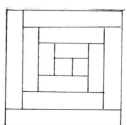 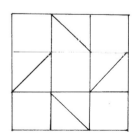

A Trapper of Today

Gary Wilder of Odgen, Utah, is an expert on most facets of the bygone trapping era. His tools, gear and clothing are replicas of the mountain man's equipment of 180 years ago. He has tanned, sinew-sewn, carved, quilled, and beaded nearly everything in this photo.

There is a national resurgence of interest in authentic reenactments of the fur rendezvous: in 1988 the Uintah Mountains Fur Rendezvous was attended by 20,000 people of all ages.

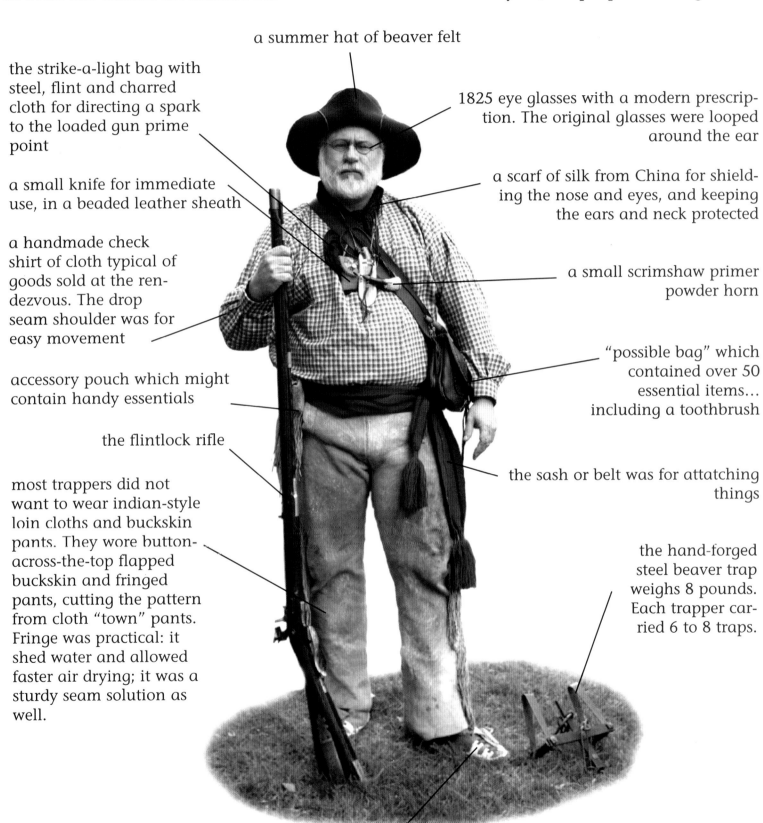

a summer hat of beaver felt

the strike-a-light bag with steel, flint and charred cloth for directing a spark to the loaded gun prime point

a small knife for immediate use, in a beaded leather sheath

a handmade check shirt of cloth typical of goods sold at the rendezvous. The drop seam shoulder was for easy movement

accessory pouch which might contain handy essentials

the flintlock rifle

most trappers did not want to wear indian-style loin cloths and buckskin pants. They wore button-across-the-top flapped buckskin and fringed pants, cutting the pattern from cloth "town" pants. Fringe was practical: it shed water and allowed faster air drying; it was a sturdy seam solution as well.

1825 eye glasses with a modern prescription. The original glasses were looped around the ear

a scarf of silk from China for shielding the nose and eyes, and keeping the ears and neck protected

a small scrimshaw primer powder horn

"possible bag" which contained over 50 essential items… including a toothbrush

the sash or belt was for attatching things

the hand-forged steel beaver trap weighs 8 pounds. Each trapper carried 6 to 8 traps.

the sinew-sewn, buckskin, pucker toe moccasin

LEATHERIZING PAPER

(making paper look like leather or buckskin)

This technique works well with brown paper grocery bags, brown wrapping paper, butcher paper and school craft paper. Newsprint does not work.

Crayons: Use any brown, rust, or orange, peeled, crayon-ends and cover your paper by coloring in big scribbles. The more layers of color, the better the "leather" look. If you have oil pastel crayons add their richness by making a few big lines. Blend the waxy colors by rubbing hard with a paper towel, your fingers or a soft rag.

Paint: Make a paint palette with a paper plate by putting a dab of each color of tempera or acrylics (acrylics are in brown, ocher, and burnt sienna) on it. Using a damp sponge dip its flat part picking up all the colors. Pick-up quite a bit of paint on the sponge. Dab the painty sponge in quick movements onto a section of your paper. Keep sponging on the paint and blend as you go. You might want a ruddy, uneven look or smooth and blended ''leather.''

Spattering: flicking specs of dark paint from dry bristles gives another "aged" texture to the leather. It is messy so do it outside or protect the surfaces around you.

THE COWPONY

We offer this paper pony project for readers that enjoy horses.

Materials: a manila file folder, natural or fanciful yarn for tail and mane, pencil, scissors, crayons, scotch tape.

1.Trim the label strip from the edge of the file folder making the edges even.

2. Transfer patterns that you have made of cowpony, saddle and blanket to the manila folder.

3. Cut out two thicknesses of cowpony, saddle and blanket.

4. Complete parts of the saddle. You may decorate your saddle to look like hand-tooled leather.

5. Cut two yards of yarn for the tail and mane. Tape to the inside of one cowpony. Use the remaining yarn for head top and bridal reins. Tape to inside.

6. Connect two sides of cowpony, blanket and saddle. You are ready to saddle up your cowpony.

7. Using your cowpony directory, choose what color your cowpony will be. Complete the horn, cantle, fenders, stirrups and cinch of the saddle and decorate the saddle blanket.

THE COWPONY DIRECTORY

Cowponies are described as being a certain color. Here is an explantion of these color terms:

PARTS OF A COWPONY

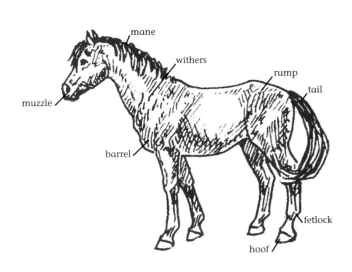

Bay is reddish brown with black points.

Appaloosa is white with small black, brown or auburn spots.

Buckskin is tan with black or brown points.

Chestnut is reddish brown all over.

Roan is white hair over dark skin color, blue roan is black skin or sorrel-reddish or amber.

PARTS OF A SADDLE

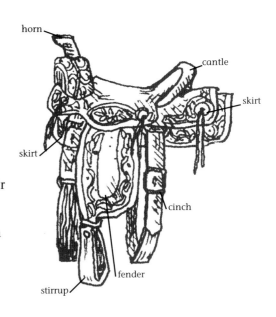

AMERICAN INDIAN DOLL PATTERN (refer to activity page 25).

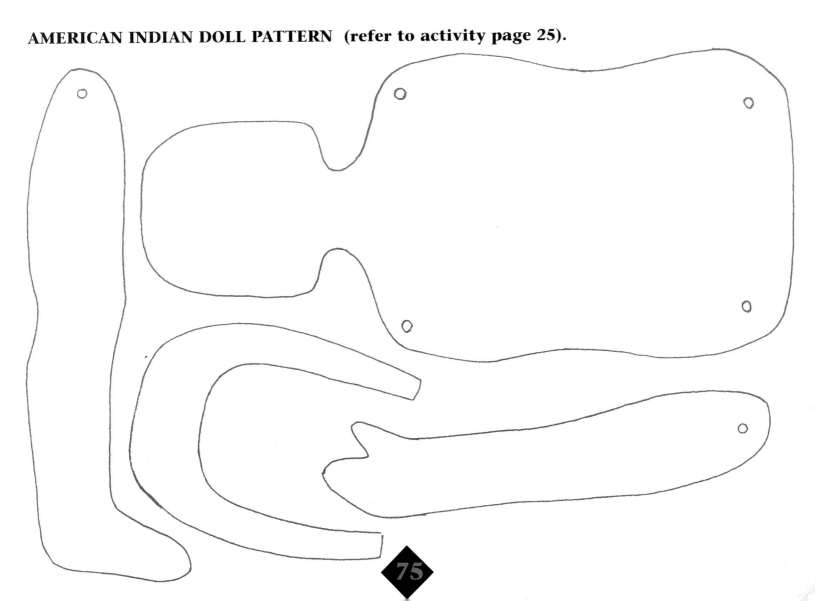

PATTERN PAGES

PUCKER TOE MOCCASIN
(refer to activity page 45).

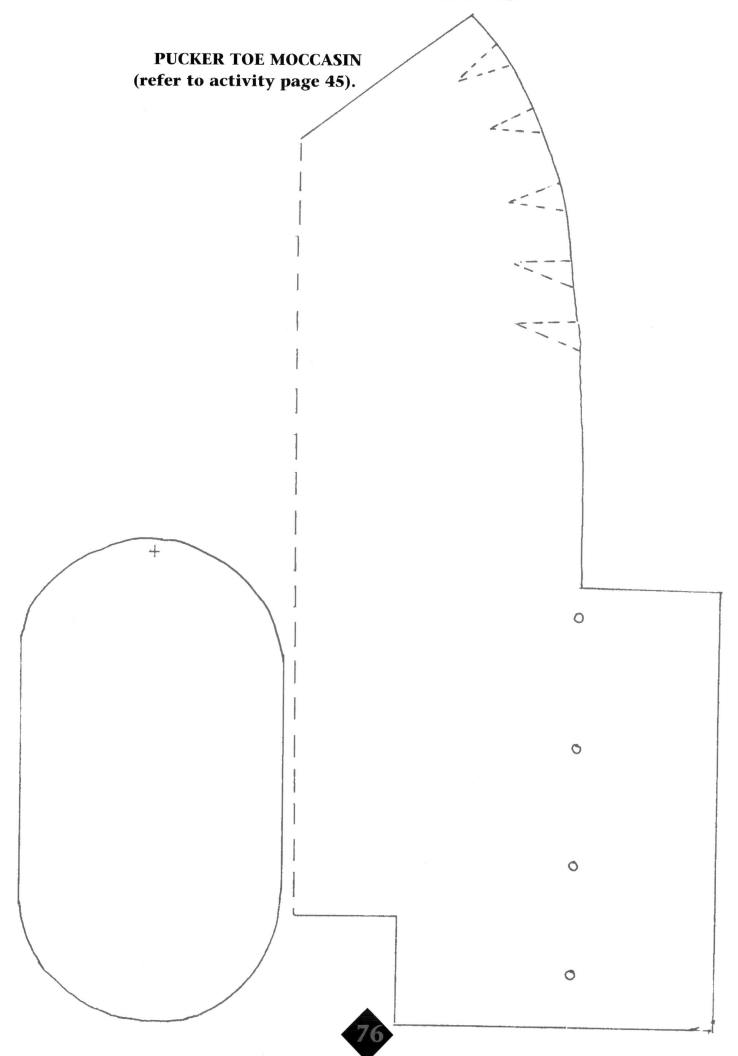

WEAVING
Continued from page 37.

3. Continue weaving around second side with over one, under one pattern. Beat down each row of weft. Continue until you run out of weft or want to change colors.

4. Overlap three or four warp threads to add a new color in the same over and under pattern as the last weft and continue. Beat down. Add new colors whenever you wish.

Your bag is finished when there is not enough space to weave any more weft. Bend the loom slots and slip off your warp threads. Pull your bag off the loom. Trim ends. Add a loop and button closure or yarn ties.

When the Spanish brought sheep to New Mexico around 1600, Navajos began weaving wool textiles. Early blankets were mostly striped and restricted to natural wool colors such as white, black, and brown. Resourceful Navajos later unravelled, respun, and dyed trade cloth, flannel underwear, and military uniforms. Mexican cochineal from the crushed shells of insects was the prized red dye. Blue indigo and other plant dyes were used as well. Navajo blanket designs are geometric and striped with the top half mirroring the bottom half.

SOME AMERICAN INDIAN SIGN LANGUAGE

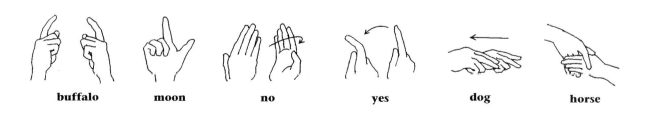

buffalo   **moon**   **no**   **yes**   **dog**   **horse**

POWDER HORN
Continued from page 43.

8. After the powder horn has cooled paint it to look like horn by mixing a little brown into your white paint. Brush it on, then rub it in. Decorate the tip with gold or black. There are three connections to the shoulder strap:

First connection:
Braid an 8 inch
string of colorful
yarn for attaching the tip of horn
to the shoulder strap. Add a decorative bead here. Attach
braided length from end of tip to shoulder strap (A)

Second connection:
Connect straps at base end of the horn and at scored tip (B).

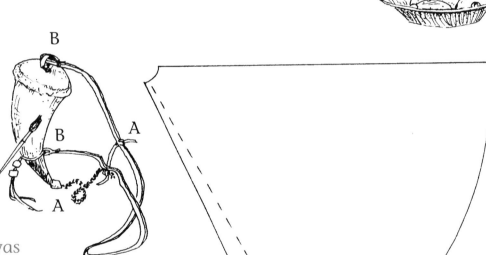

The trappers most
important accessory was
his rifle. It was never far from
his side. Some guns even had pet names.
Early trappers used the flintlock rifle. The flintlock fired on the principle of flint striking against
steel. The two powder horns, the small primer and
the larger horn, were both essential to fuel the flintlock. The gun was also known as the Kentucky or the
Lancaster long rifle.

The Hawken was another popular gun tho it was too expensive
for most mountain men. The Hawken needed a shooting bag.
This buckskin pouch carried balls, patches, powder, lead and bullet molds.

ACKNOWLEGMENTS

To the following people and organizations, I express my heartfelt appreciation for assisting
with the content and emphasis of this book:

Kay Jones, a Salt Lake City art teacher, for her valuable suggestions at the right developmental stage of research and production; **Nancy Matthews,** Social Studies Coordinator for Utah State Office of Education and **Jeanne Moe,** National Project Archaeology Coordinator, Burea of Land Management, who previewed the text for content accuracy with special attention to the Early People. The technical and literary quality of the text was reviewed by **Madlyn Tanner. Emily Mortensen** shared her insights and writing talent throughout the book. **Dorothy Graham** loaned her library resources. Jordan School District Administrators in the Bi-lingual program previewed the book content.

The Utah Museum of Natural History generously provided the knowledge and artifacts supervised by **Laurel Casjens,** Curator of Collections, and **Kathy Kankainen,** Curator of Anthropology. These pieces are featured in the Early People and American Indian units. The **T.P. Gallery** in Salt Lake City loaned the Ute and Navajo dolls. **Linda Harrelson** crafted the doll with grey braids wearing a costume of traditional and western clothing. **Harold Garce** created the Ute doll with traditional beading. **Will Numkena** of the Bureau of Indian Affairs previewed the material for the American Indian unit. The Trapper unit represents hours of time and knowledge shared by **Julie and Gary Wilder.**

Doris Gillette loaned us her heirloom quilt. The Cowboy unit had assistance from The Chase Home Museum of Utah Folk Art, **Carol Edison,** Folk Art Coordinator and **Anne Hatch,** assistant Folk Art Coordinator. The cowboy unit was generously outfitted with old and new objects from A.A.Callister Co., a Western gear and clothing store in Utah. Our thanks to **Ned Callister** and **MaryAnn Knaphus,** co-owners. **Dennis Manning** in Roosevelt, Utah still makes the Mormon hobbles. **Jay Sharp** loaned us his hand-forged horseshoe hammer and **Jerry Stewart** of Vernal, Utah made the sawtooth custom working saddle from a turn-of-the-century model. Our horseshoes were made by **Mike Majera** of the Utah Horseshoers Guild.

General References:

Ellsworth, Geo. S. *Utah's Heritage.* Salt Lake City, Utah: Gibbs Smith, 1992. Utah State Historical Society. *The History Blazer.* Salt Lake City, Utah: 1995. Reader's Digest Assoc. *Story of the Great American West.* Pleasantville, New York: 1972. Reedstrom, E. Lisle. *Authentic Costumes and Characters of the Wild West.* New York: Sterling, 1992. Bergin and Steedman. *A Frontier Fort on the Oregon Trail.* New York: Peter Bedrick Books, 1993. Ord, John and Susan Stone. *The Student Reader Series.* Provo, Utah: Council Press, 1981.

Early People References:

Moe, Jeanne. *Intrigue of the Past: Investigating Archaeology.* Bureau of Land Management, Dept. of Interior, Salt Lake City, Utah: Seagull Printing, 1992. *The Anasazi,* Southwest Natural and Cultural Heritage Assn.(SNCHA). Utah: 1992. *The Anasazi,* SNCHA, 1992. Zimmerman, Mary Ann. *Utah Prehistory.* Murray, Utah: Jordan School District, 1987. Bergosh, Jerry and Jeanne Moe. *Rock Art of Utah.* Tuscon, Arizona: Salix Corporation, 1995. *Anasazi.* Tuscon, Arizona: Southwest Parks and Monuments Assoc. (SPMA),1992. Fuller. *Anasazi, Builders of Wonders.* Fuller, 1991. Utah Museum of Natural History, *Treading in the Past: Sandals of the Anasazi.* Salt Lake City, Utah: UMNH Press, 1995.

American Indian References:

Baylor, Byrd and Tom Bahti.*When Clay Sings.* New York: Aladdin Books, 1972. Cohlene, Terri and Charles Reasoner. *Turquoise Boy: A Navajo Legend.* Vero Beach, Florida: Watermill Press, 1990. Copeland, Peter F. *Southwest Indians Coloring Book.* New York: Dover Publications, 1994. Furst, Peter T.and Jill. *North American Indian Art.* New York: Rizzoli, 1982. Feder, Norman. *American Indian Art.* New York: Harry N. Abrams,1982. Hunt, Ben and Buck Burshears. *American Indian Beadwork.* New York: Collier Books, 1951. Hunt, W. Ben. *Indian Crafts and Lore.* New York: Golden Press, 1964. McQuiston, Don and Debra. *Dolls and Toys of Native America.* San Fransisco: Chronicle Books, 1995. Thompson, Paul. *Indians of Utah.* Alpine, Utah: North Mountain Publishing Company, 1988. Rand McNally. *Children's Atlas of Native Americans.* Chicago: R.M., 1992. Time-Life Books. *The Indians.* TLB, 1973. Time-Life Books. *The Great Chiefs.* TLB, 1975. Walker Art Center. *American Indian Art: Form and Tradition.* New York: Dutton, 1972.

Trapper References:

Time-Life Books. *The Frontiersmen.* Time-Life Books, 1977. Utah State Historical Society. *Beehive History.* Salt Lake City, Utah: 1975. Time-Life Books. *The Trailblazers.* TLB, 1973.

Settler References:

Merrill, Yvonne Young. *Hands-on Pioneers.* Salt Lake City, Utah: Deseret Publishing, 1995. Paxman, Shirley. *Homespun.* Salt Lake City, Utah: Deseret Book Co.,1976. Utah State Historical Society. *Beehive Histories: Community Life.* Salt Lake City, Utah: USHS, 1985. Time-Life Books. *The Pioneers.* TLB, 1974. Thompson, Paul. *Pioneers of Utah.* Alpine, Utah: NMPC, 1988.

Cowboy References:

Morris, Michele. *The Cowboy Life.* New York: Fireside Press, 1993. Time-Life Books. *The Cowboys.* New York: TLB, 1973. Mcquery,Rod and Sue Wallis. *The Whole Cowboy Catalog.* Salt Lake City, Utah: Gibbs Smith Publishing, 1995.

INDEX

PHOTO KEY

EARLY PEOPLE ARTIFACTS PHOTO KEY
The artifacts in this photograph are from the collection of the Utah Museum of Natural History.

The primary resource materials that were molded, woven, chipped, painted, and carved by prehistory man used yucca plant parts, animal skins, clay, charcoal, chert, obsidian, wood, bone and horn.

1. Fremont bowl of grey clay with painted black designs
2. woven tray of dried yucca fibers
3. Anasazi red clay painted jug
4. a hank of spun cotton
5. rabbit skin from Anasazi period
6. painted mug from Fremont people
7. pictoglyph figure painted on a rock
8. dried yucca leaves
9. yucca cordage
10. grey clay figurines by Fremont
11. shards from grey pottery of mixed origin
12. chert projectile tip
13. obsidian projectile tips
14. yucca fiber woven basket
15. wooden spindle for spinning fibers
16. bone awl, and other bone tools

AMERICAN INDIAN ARTIFACTS PHOTO KEY
The artifacts in this photograph are from the collection of the Utah Museum of Natural History.

1. Navajo wedding basket
2. Navajo child wearing blanket
3. Ute story robe
4. Bannock beaded pouch
5. Apache beaded pouch
6. Paiute beaded gloves
7. Ute doll cradle board
8. beaded coin purse
9. beaded arm band
10. whistle made of bird bone
11. flap beaded pouch
12. Sioux parfleche with quill work
13. Ute beaded moccasin
14. beaded moccasin
15. beaded baby moccasins

TRAPPER PHOTO KEY

1. knife sheath with Mandan American Indian influence
2. Lewis and Clark Expedition medallion presented to chiefs and prized by them
3. French blue knit voyageur hat
4. parfleche saddle bag
5. stretched beaver hide on willow frame
6. large bone scraper for hide and small scraper
7. wooden holder of castor gland called a 'castoreum'
8. buffalo bladder water bottle
9. sinew
10. sheath
11. antler buttons
12. beaded strap for hat or attachments
13. beaver trap
14. red fox winter hat
15. possible bag
16. large powder horn
17. small powder horn
18. beaver voucher medal which served as money at rendezous
19. trade money mixed with antler buttons
20. bone comb
21. pig bristle and bone toothbrush
22. mud turtle pouch
23. horn spoon
24. handmade scissors
25. beaded bag used as a strike-a-light (fire starter materials)
26. high fashion beaver hat from Europe
27. pucker toe moccasin with shearling lining
28. trappers woven basket
29. beaver felt hat for summer wear
30. handcrafted snowshoe
31. parfleche saddle bag
32. parfleche quiver that held tinder for fire starting
33. Ute traded beaded bag for medicines and herbs

The items in the Trapper photograph are from the collection of Gary and Julie Wilder.

COWBOY PHOTO KEY

Cowboy gear has changed very little in design and function since the cowboy heyday. Today, however the western look is fashionable and boots, outfits, hats and jewelry have become popular with women and men, teens and children. Most would agree that blue denim is one of the fabrics and styles worn by people in every nation. It all started with the cowboy and his comfortable, body-fitting working blue jeans.

1. handcrafted saddle
2. dress hat of white felt with a braided horsehair band
3. traditional lariat
4. dress leather boot
5. working leather gloves
6. bandanna
7. horseshoes
8. Mormon hobbles: these steel hobbles release with a trick in working the metal chain. They are still made and used.
9. stirrup
10. Appaloosa pony statue
11. plastic dentalium beads, silver and leather belt.
12. breaking-the-horse head gear to control head movement
13. horsehair and sisal striped decorative rope
14. enlarged buffalo nickel belt buckle

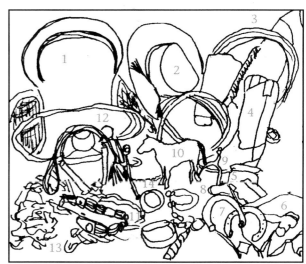